DELPHI

in easy steps

BRENDAN MURPHY

COMPUTER
STEP

In easy steps is an imprint of Computer Step
Southfield Road . Southam
Warwickshire CV47 OFB . England

http://www.ineasysteps.com

Notice of Liability

Every effort has been made to ensure that this book contains accurate
and current information. However, Computer Step and the author shall
not be liable for any loss or damage suffered by readers as a result of
any information contained herein.

Trademarks

All Inprise and Borland brand names are trademarks or registered
trademarks of Inprise Corporation. All other trademarks are
acknowledged as belonging to their respective companies.

Printed and bound in the United Kingdom

ISBN 1-84078-115-7

Contents

4 Basic Programming Skills 57

5 Using Database Tables 75

6 Writing Reports 89

Getting Started

This chapter will introduce you to Delphi and explain the versions of the software commonly in use. You will learn how to install and open Delphi and you will create, run and save your first project. You'll also be introduced to the Object Inspector and the Component Palette and look at the structure of a Delphi project as well as finding out how you can find help should you run into problems.

Covers

Chapter One

Introduction

Earlier versions of Delphi can often be found on the free CDs that accompany popular computer magazines.

Delphi is a rapid application development tool that allows you to quickly build computer programs that will run in the Windows environment. With Delphi you can create personal and business applications quickly and effectively and these applications can be distributed 'royalty-free' without worry. Delphi makes computer programming easy as all of the work is carried out in the Integrated Development Environment (IDE). The IDE acts like an artist's canvass allowing you to visually see how your finished program will look. Delphi is an excellent tool for building database applications and it can link to all the major Windows-based database systems.

Delphi Professional edition has all the functionality of the Standard edition. The Enterprise edition has all the functionality of the Professional edition.

Delphi is available in the following versions:

- Standard: entry level product offering a quick method of creating Windows applications. Extensive use of wizards makes programming easy for the beginner. Incorporates over 80 reusable components including automation components for MS Office allowing applications to be integrated with Word, Excel, PowerPoint and Outlook.

Delphi version 1.0 is 16-bit. This means that it was designed for older PCs. Applications built using Delphi 2.0 and above (32-bit), will not run on PCs running the 16-bit Windows 3.11 environment. Any application built using Delphi 1.0 will happily run on all versions of Windows.

- Professional: productive Windows development tool for the design and operation of database and Web-based applications. Incorporating a professional IDE and robust debugging tools. Over 150 reusable objects makes programming fast and professional.

- Enterprise: high-end product for developing database and Web-based applications. Comes with over 200 reusable components in a visual component library to allow rapid application development. Also shipped with a suite of enhanced management and productivity tools. Supports Oracle 8i.

Installing Delphi

Install Delphi first. You can always come back and install other applications at a later date.

To install Delphi, insert the installation CD into your PC and the installation screen will automatically load. (If the autorun option doesn't work on your system you can run the INSTALL.EXE file from your CD to begin the process.) You will be given the opportunity to choose which product you wish to install.

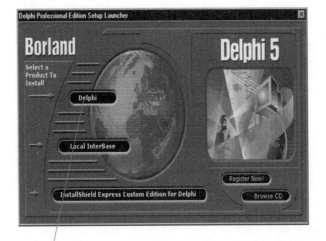

Delphi Professional edition takes up nearly 200MB of hard disk space. Delphi Standard edition takes up over 100MB of disk space. Make sure there is enough free space on your hard disc before installing Delphi.

1 Choose Delphi. The Local InterBase option is for advanced use and can be left unchecked. The InstallShield Express application is a useful utility that enables easy distribution of your completed applications. (Not available in the Standard Edition.)

To create more space on your hard disc, empty your Recycle Bin regularly. Make sure any temp files (.tmp extension) are also cleared from your hard disc.

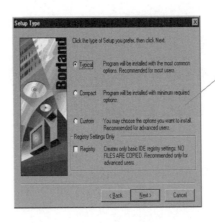

2 Choose the type of install. Unless you're an advanced user, choose 'Typical'.

You will now be guided through the Delphi setup process. If the setup program detects any files that are currently on your PC that have a file type used by Delphi, you will be asked whether these should be automatically associated with Delphi.

File Associations work in Windows Explorer. Agreeing to associate particular file types with Delphi will mean that opening them in Windows Explorer will open the associated Delphi program.

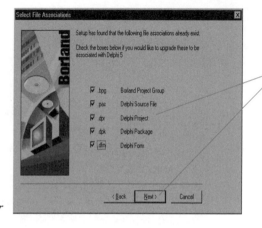

3 Check any boxes that you want to associate with Delphi.

If you use other Borland products, then do not change the default directory of shared files during Delphi setup. If you do, you risk these products not working properly when you next run them.

You will now be guided through the remainder of the setup process. The setup program will ask you to make some more decisions and will give you default suggestions for things like program groups and folders to hold the Delphi system files. Unless you have some specific reason for not choosing these, it's always best to accept the suggestions offered.

If you wish to install any of the other programs that are available on the Delphi CD you can do this now before re-booting your PC. (Professional and Enterprise versions only.)

4 When Delphi has finished installing you must re-boot your PC before using the program.

Starting Delphi

As with most applications that run under Windows, Delphi can be started in a number of ways. You should make any appropriate changes to your Windows settings to ensure that Delphi starts the way that best suits your normal operation.

By right-clicking on the Delphi icon in the Delphi menu, you can send a short-cut to your PC desktop allowing easy start-up.

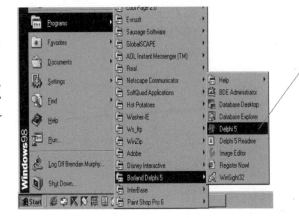

Use the Start button and access the Programs menu. Under the Delphi option choose the Delphi icon.

2 If a Delphi short-cut has been setup, start Delphi by double-clicking on the icon on the Windows desktop or the Delphi icon found in the Delphi folder.

Delphi

Quickly find the path for the Delphi icon by using the Windows Find program to search for the DELPHI32.EXE file.

3 You can start Delphi by accessing it through the My Computer icon on your desktop. Simply double-click through the Programs icon on the C drive until you reach the Borland folder. From here, you should easily find the Delphi icon (see the Hot Tip if you can't find the Delphi icon).

A first look at the Delphi IDE

When you start Delphi the first screen that will open will be the Delphi IDE. From here, you can use a number of the major tools used when developing applications in Delphi.

All components used in Delphi, including forms, are objects.

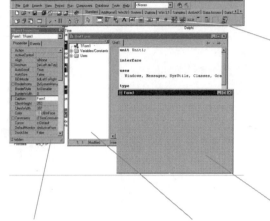

The Component Palette. A library of ready-made components that can be used in your application.

Objects are inherited from classes. Each object is an instance of its ancestor class – it is a descendent and incorporates all the functionality of the class it is derived from. Polymorphism means that different objects derived from the same ancestor support the same functionality.

The Object Inspector. Changes an object's properties and its function.

The Code Explorer. Allows you to quickly navigate through the code in each Delphi unit.

The Form Designer. This is where you visually build your applications.

Where they all fit

- Forms. Your completed Delphi application will be made up of a number of windows. These are known as forms and they each contain a number of components.

- Components. These are the buttons, menus, fields, database controls and other building blocks that create the finished visual look of a Windows-based application.

- Program Code. Program Code is the name given to the instructions that you write as a programmer to allow your application to do something useful when it is run.

- Object. An object is a data type that holds both data and operations on that data in a single unit.

Adding a button

When you first start Delphi you will be presented with Form1. This is the first form for your new application and it is where you'll use components to build a working system. One of the most popular components used to build applications are buttons. Delphi has a number of different button types, the simplest being a basic button found in the Standard component tab of the Component Palette.

 Press F11 to display the Object Inspector for the highlighted component. If no component is highlighted, the Object Inspector relates to the current form.

Placing a button on your form

| Click on the OK button.

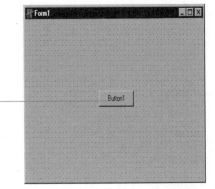

 You can move the button around the form by dragging it, and resize it by clicking on one of its handles and dragging to the desired size.

2 Click anywhere on the form and a new button, named Button1, will be placed on the form.

The Object Inspector for Button1 should now be displayed. This allows you to make changes to the look and operation of the button.

 You can also add a component from the Component List in the View Menu. This method also offers a component search facility.

Compiling and running your project

Now that you've created a new project and added a button to your first form, you are ready to compile and run this project. Compiling a computer program takes the code that you have written and turns it into machine code – a language that the computer understands. During this process, any errors are reported to you. After successful compilation an executable (EXE) file is created that can then be run.

Each time you run your project, Delphi will automatically re-compile if any changes have been made since your last compilation.

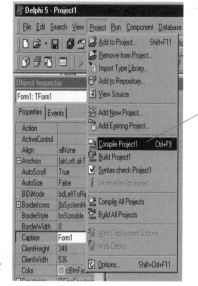

From the Project menu, choose Compile. Alternatively, press Ctrl+F9.

As your project becomes bigger it's a good idea to regularly run the Build command from the Project menu. Building a project re-compiles the complete project irrespective of whether any changes have been made since the last compilation.

2 To run your project simply choose Run from the Run menu. Alternatively, press F9 or choose the Run icon from the toolbar.

The Run icon

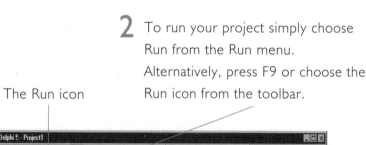

A first look at the Object Inspector

The Object Inspector is the place where you can decide how each component in your application both looks and operates. The Object Inspector allows you to set design-time properties for components you have placed on each form as well as setting the properties of the form itself.

The object selector at the top of the Object Inspector is a drop-down list containing all the components on the active form and it also displays the object type of the selected component. This lets you quickly display properties and events for the different components on the current form.

'Design-time properties' are those properties set in the Object Inspector when you are developing, rather than running, your Delphi application.

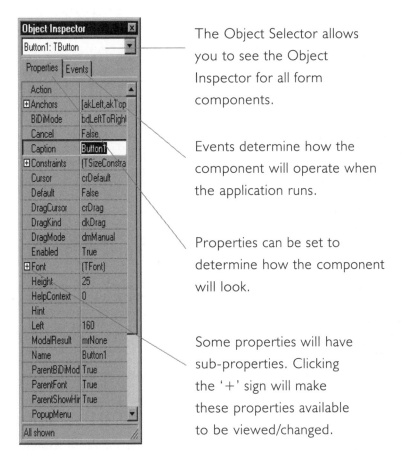

The Object Selector allows you to see the Object Inspector for all form components.

Events determine how the component will operate when the application runs.

Properties can be set to determine how the component will look.

Some properties will have sub-properties. Clicking the '+' sign will make these properties available to be viewed/changed.

The properties and events that a component will have will depend on the object and class that it is associated with. Buttons have the following common properties and events:

Properties

• Caption – the text displayed on the button.

• Font – the font used for the button caption.

• Enabled – determines if users can press the button.

• Hint – text when the mouse is placed over the button.

• Visible – sets if the button will be visible at run-time.

Events

• OnClick – the code behind this event will run when the button is pressed.

• OnEnter – the code behind this event will run when the user tabs onto the button.

• OnExit – the code behind this event will run when the user tabs off the button.

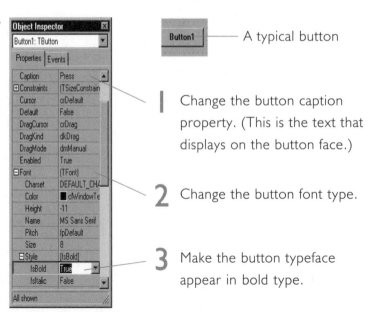

A typical button

1 Change the button caption property. (This is the text that displays on the button face.)

2 Change the button font type.

3 Make the button typeface appear in bold type.

Adding code to your button

Create a new Delphi project and place a button onto Form1. If you compile and run this project nothing will happen. To make the button actually perform a function requires that you place some code behind it. This is known as 'adding an event' to the button.

When you add components to forms, Delphi automatically names them.
Your first task should be to change the Name property of each component to a meaningful name.

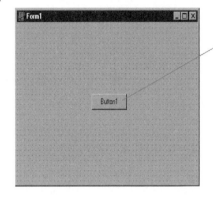

1 Create a new project and place a button onto Form1.

2 Change the Name property of the button to read 'btnPress'.

You can also access the button's OnClick event through choosing it in the Events tab of the Object Inspector.

3 Double-click on the button to open the OnClick event. Add the following code between the 'begin' and 'end'.

You can toggle between viewing your form, and the program code behind it, using the F12 key.

4 From the Run menu, run the program (it will compile automatically) and press the button on your form. Watch what happens – the button caption changes!

For every form you create in a Delphi application, an associated unit is created and this is where the actual program code that does the work is held. Within each unit, little procedures are stored, each relating to an event in each component's Object Inspector (in the Events tab). In the button example, you added code to the OnClick event for the button setting it up to run this code when the button is pressed. The actual program code entered is written in Object Pascal:

The code behind components in Delphi is written in Pascal. Having a basic understanding of Pascal helps when using Delphi , but is not essential.

```
begin
    btnPress.Caption:='Just press me';
end;
```

The caption 'Just press me' is assigned(:=) to the property Caption belonging to the btnPress component. You can read this as "the button's caption becomes 'Just press me'."

When you view the code for a component you will notice that some words are in a bold typeface. Delphi shows reserved words (words that have a special meaning to the language) in bold. If you amend any of these words you will get a program error.

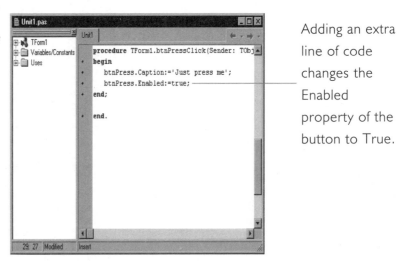

Adding an extra line of code changes the Enabled property of the button to True.

When you compile and run your program you may see an error message. If this happens, check your code. You're almost sure to have made a mistake entering it.

You can change the values of component properties either at design-time or at run-time. Design-time refers to changing properties within the Object Inspector when you are working within the Delphi IDE, run-time refers to changing the properties of a component program through program code when you run the program – as in the above example.

A first look at the Component Palette

The Component Palette provides you with a wealth of components that can be used in your Delphi applications. Components are split into categories, each category has an associated page and an access tab for quick entry.

Components can either be visual or non-visual. Visual components (e.g. buttons) can be seen when the application is running, whilst non-visual components (e.g. Timer) are not seen at run-time. All components are visible at design-time.

Component page tabs

To find out what each component does, place your mouse over the component icon for just over one second and then read the hint shown.

Scroll for more page tabs.

You can add a new page tab within the Component Palette (context menu) and drag the most used components to this new page for ease of use.

2 Right-click anywhere on the Component Palette and amend the context menu entries. These entries provide help for the components listed, allow you to enable/disable icon hints and hide the Component Palette as well as change the order in which components are displayed on the palette.

A first look at units

Forms are the visible face of Delphi and are easily manipulated by changing properties in the Object Inspector and by adding components. However, form 'units' are where the actual program code instructions that you enter are held. Every Delphi form has an associated unit which contains the source code for all the events attached to the components displayed on the form. Delphi helps you when building applications by self-generating most of the source code for you.

Each form has only one unit. This means that every piece of code entered in component events are stored in one file.

You can toggle between the form and its unit using F12.

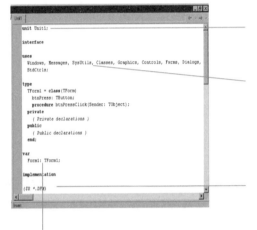

Unit name.

Units that already exist and are used by this one.

The actual code you enter for component events follows in the implementation section.

Declaration of the classes that the form and components are descendents of. Declaration of any component event headers.

Every Delphi application includes a controlling unit that is self-generated and named after the project name that you choose for your application.

As your Delphi applications become bigger, more forms and more units will exist. Delphi provides an easy way to keep track of, and navigate to, these units.

Click on the View Unit icon to view all units associated with your project.

Saving your project

When you write computer programs for distribution these are normally called applications. In Delphi, however, each program is known as a project. Projects should be created and stored in separate folders within your PC to enable easy management and distribution when they are completed.

Always create a new project folder for each of your applications and save all your project files here. Failing to do this can cause you major problems later.

Use File, Save regularly as you work. This will save any changes to the current unit displayed in the IDE.

Give your project a meaningful name. Delphi will save any unsaved units at this point, again, prompting you for a unit name.

If you save a unit to the wrong folder by mistake, move it using Windows Explorer and change the path that points to the unit in the main controlling project unit.

Use File, Save As to copy a version of each unit and associated form to another folder on your PC.

There is no requirement in Delphi to save your form files. These are automatically saved each time you save the corresponding unit – or the project as a whole. Also, remember to choose a different name for your unit file to the name chosen in the Name property of the associated form's Object Inspector – form and unit names must be unique.

The terms 'project' and 'application' can be considered synonymous in Delphi.

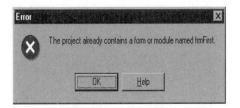

Reopening your project

Once you've created and successfully stored your Delphi project, the next important task is to be able to easily reopen this project to allow further additions and amendments to be made to it.

The File, Open command can be used to open single units as well as complete projects.

Method 1

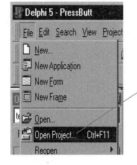

Choose the Open Project menu item. Then simply locate and open the required Delphi project.

You can quickly open a Delphi project using Ctrl+F11.

Method 2

Delphi provides a useful function for project management. When you close a project, it is added to the Reopen list. The Reopen list can contain up to a maximum of five projects.

Projects are only listed in the Reopen list if they were closed using File, Close.

| Choose the File, Reopen menu item to see a drop down list of recently worked on projects.

Delphi can only have one project open at any one time. Make sure you save all your changes before closing a project and opening a new one.

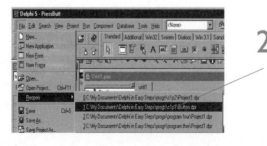

2 Choose the desired project from the list shown.

Delphi project files

Each Delphi project is made up of a number of files. As far as you are concerned the only two file types that you actually create are units and forms. However, Delphi self generates a number of other files all used to create a finished project:

To ensure that your Delphi applications work correctly, make any changes to the DPR file through the Project Manager (View, Project Manager).

- DPR file. This is the Delphi project file (controlling unit) and it contains details of all the units and forms used in your project. This file is self generated by Delphi. You can amend the contents of the DPR file through viewing it as a unit.

- CFG file. The Project configuration file stores settings for your project. It has the same name as your project but with the extension .CFG.

- DOF file. This is the Delphi options file. It contains the settings made when you change the Project Options dialogue box via the Project, Options menu item.

- RES file. This file contains information about the Delphi version being used to create the project as well as holding the main icon for the project.

- EXE file. The executable file is created when you compile your project. This file is used to run your completed project. It has the same name as the project with the extension .EXE.

- DFM file. This is the Delphi form file. One will be created for each form in your project and it contains technical information about the placing of components and the general look of the form.

- PAS file. This is a Delphi unit file and it contains the code to carry out tasks (events) required on each form. Every form has an associated unit file.

Viewing Delphi project files

To view Delphi project files you can use the View menu's Project Manager. Or you can use Windows Explorer to locate and view the files in the associated project folder.

Getting help

Delphi is an excellent programming language that makes complex tasks easy. However, it is a programming language, and as such has many rules that must be followed. It is therefore useful to know how and where to get help.

The Internet provides a great source of Delphi help. Use a search engine such as Google (www.google.com), and enter the keyword 'Delphi'.

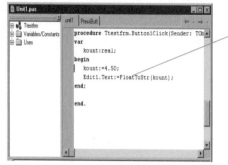

Place your cursor on the word/command you need help with. Press F1.

2 A pop-up window will appear giving help on the word/command requested.

Help is also available from the Help menu in the Delphi IDE. You can search by topic, or by keyword.

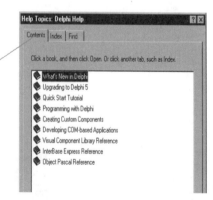

Using Components

This chapter will introduce you to methods and how they interact with component properties/events. You will also find out how to add a host of standard components to your Delphi application.

Covers

Chapter Two

Methods, properties and events

Each component has a visible image which is seen on each form when you place the component. However components also have properties, events and methods. In chapter one we looked briefly at properties and events, now you will consider the importance of methods.

Methods

Methods are procedures and functions that operate on components, they carry out an instruction. You can instruct components to execute one of these procedures or functions (methods) at run-time only. Unlike events, methods are provided for you by the Delphi environment itself. They do not require you to write any code whatsoever and this helps you greatly as methods are complex and would be difficult to code (one of the benefits of using the Delphi IDE). A typical method for a button (named Button1) is:

button1.Hide;

(This method hides the button by changing its visible property to False.)

If you want to test whether a button can have control passed to it, you must check that both its Enabled and Visible property are set to True. You could call the following:

button1.CanFocus;

If this method returns True then the button can receive control.

Properties

Properties allow you to change certain aspects of a component's look and operation. Properties are easy to change via the Object Inspector; changes are instantly seen.

Events

An event is a special property that causes some program code to run at run-time. This code is written by you.

Using command buttons

Buttons are used to allow the user to instigate an event. A button might be used to close a form, or to enable you to proceed to the next form in a system, or to print the current form. Buttons can also be used as menu items allowing a choice to be made from a number of options.

When you add a button to a form the Caption and Name properties are the same. Change the Name property to be more meaningful.

Add the '&' sign in front of any letter in a button's caption. Then use Alt+letter, to pass focus to the button and run the OnClick event.

Look in the Additional component tab for two further buttons, BitBtn and SpeedButton. These buttons are basic buttons with extra properties such as having the ability to add a graphic to the button face.

Unless otherwise stated, all components used in this chapter can be found in the Standard or Additional component tab.

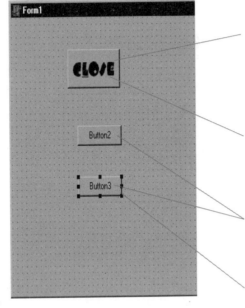

Change the Caption property to change the text displayed.

Change the Font property and the caption text font will change.

Buttons are sequentially named when added to a form.

Resize a button by dragging its handles.

Button events

The following events can be coded behind the button's OnClick event.

Closing the active form.

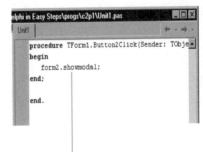

Opening another form.

Using edit and memo boxes

Edit components allow you to capture information typed in by the user. Memo components are similar to Edit components, the main difference being that multiple lines of text can be captured using them.

Edit boxes can be used to simply display text to the user. This is useful if this text requires to be copied or cut into the Windows clipboard.

An Edit component.

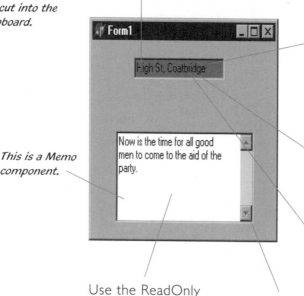

Change the Color property to amend the Edit component's background colour.

The CharCase property allows you to specify if the Edit component will accept normal text.

This is a Memo component.

The MaxLength property lets you limit the number of inserted characters.

Use the ReadOnly property to display text only.

The ScrollBars property allows vertical and horizontal scrolling.

Edit and Memo component events

The following events can be coded behind the Edit component's OnChange event and the Memo component's OnClick event. Note that the Memo component has a Lines property (with the square brackets after it). This indicates that you are assigning the value of Edit1.Text into the first line of the memo component.

Each component has a number of events associated with it, and any of the code listed on the next page could have been put behind these events.

This example shows the ability to affect the properties of one component (the button) from the event handler executed in a different component (the edit component).

Button1's caption property is changed from the OnChange event of the Edit box.

The first line of the Memo box will have a message displayed when the user clicks the Memo box.

How this example will look when running.

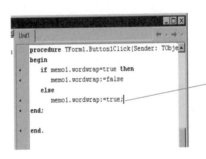

If the user clicks on the Toggle WordWrap button and the memo component's WordWrap property is True (WordWrap turned on) then it is made False. If it is True, then it is made False (switched off).

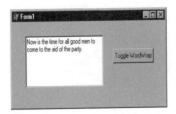

How this example will look when running.

Using Label components

Labels are used to display text that the user can neither change nor manipulate in any way. Label components often act as signposts for other components such as edit components, directing the user to completion requirements for data entry.

These are Label components.

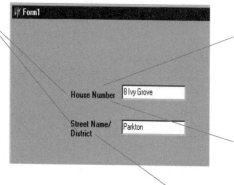

The Caption property holds the text string displayed on the label.

Labels cannot have focus in a form. Link each label's FocusControl property with an Edit component (or other component) and control will be passed to here if the user uses the Accelerator key setup in the label's Caption property.

The Font, Style property enables you to make the label bold.

The WordWrap property allows the label to take up more than one line. When the AutoSize property is set as True, the label can grow, depending on the length of text entered

Aligning Labels

A number of labels often exist on a form. Aligning these labels can be tricky when done manually, however Delphi provides an automated solution to be used.

Set the Transparent property to True and the label can then be used to 'sit on top' of another component such as an image.

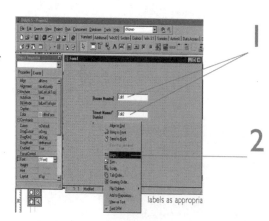

1 Select the labels to be aligned by holding down the Shift key and clicking on them.

2 Right click and choose Align. Align the labels as appropriate.

labels as appropria

Using CheckBoxes

Check boxes allow the user to include an entry on a form that allows toggling between yes and no or True and False. Check boxes are True when they are checked (ticked) and are False when left unchecked.

A CheckBox component with the Caption property changed.

The AllowGrayed property determines whether your check box will have three different states, checked, unchecked and greyed.

Align the caption to the left or right of the check box.

The Checked property is used by the programmer to determine whether the check box has been ticked by the user.

Working with CheckBoxes

1 Write this piece of program code behind the OnClick event of the CheckBox.

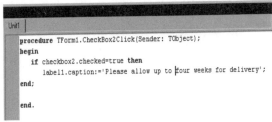

```
Unit1
procedure TForm1.CheckBox2Click(Sender: TObject);
begin
    if checkbox2.checked=true then
        label1.caption:='Please allow up to four weeks for delivery';
end;

end.
```

2 Compile and run the program. Watch the label change when you click on the check box.

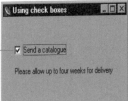

Using radio buttons and radio groups

Radio buttons are used to allow the user to make only one choice from a number of available choices. They differ from check boxes in that check boxes work independently from each other, radio boxes operate in a group of two or more.

The most popular component in Delphi for working with radio buttons is the RadioGroup component. This component groups radio buttons into sets allowing more than one group to be placed on any form.

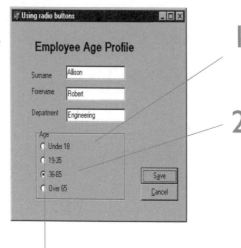

1 Place a RadioGroup component onto your form.

2 Add radio button entries by placing a list of entries in the Items property.

If you would like your radio group to take up more than one column then amend the Columns property to the appropriate number of columns required.

3 Amend the Caption property to give the group a heading.

4 Set the ItemIndex property to determine the first radio button to be active by default (0 is the first entry in your radio group).

Displaying a message from a radio button value

If you resize a radio group, each radio button in it will be repositioned accordingly.

```
Unit1
procedure TForm1.RadioGroup1Exit(Sender: TObject);
begin
   if radiogroup1.itemindex=2 then
      label5.caption:='Pension bonus opportunities available';
end;

end.
```

1 Place this program code behind the OnExit event.

2 A message displays on a label (label5) if the user chooses the 36-65 radio button. The message is displayed when control is passed to another component on the form either by clicking or tabbing off the radio group.

Using combo boxes, panels and bevels

A combo box is an edit box combined with a scrollable drop-down list. It allows the user to make a choice from a list, or type directly into the edit box with a new value.

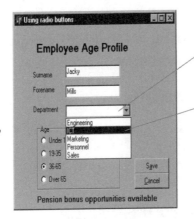

1 Place a ComboBox component onto your form.

2 Enter your list of entries into the List property.

4 Change the Style property to determine how the combo box will operate.

3 Sort the entries in the combo box alphabetically by setting the Sorted property to True.

Adding panels and bevels to your form

Panels and bevels are used to give your form a more professional look. A panel can be used to act as a container for other components. This means that as the panel is moved so are the contained components. Bevels can be used to place around fields giving a chiselled look to the form.

A Panel component with the bevel width property changed to the value two.

A Bevel component used to act as a background to two command buttons.

Using a MaskEdit

A MaskEdit is simply an edit box with rules. These rules act as a template and prevent the user entering information in a format that is unsuitable. MaskEdits offer a means of simple validation. Validation helps make your applications more robust ensuring that data entry is as error free as possible.

A MaskEdit has similar properties and events as a standard Edit component.

Creating/using a MaskEdit component with the EditMask property

Look up Delphi help for the EditMask property and find out the characters that can be used to create a custom mask such as the postcode example shown.

A MaskEdit component that accepts postcode details in the form ML6 7RT, JK3 1QE etc.

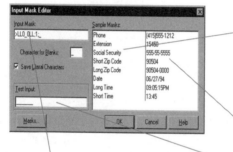

Sample mask that can be clicked and chosen.

Details of the characters used to create a mask.

You can just as easily setup a password field using a simple Edit component.

The actual mask being used.

A test area to try out the mask.

Creating a password field via a MaskEdit component

If you want to enter data into a field and not have it displayed, such as a password, then you can achieve this by using the MaskEdit component.

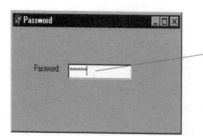

Change the PasswordChar property to a character of your choice. This character will be displayed when data is entered.

Using a DateTimePicker

The DateTimePicker component can be found on the Win32 component page. The components on the Win32 page provide access to 32-bit Windows user interface common controls available to your Delphi projects.

The DateTimePicker component allows you to easily choose a valid date/time from a form field. It displays a combo-box which, when clicked, displays an illustrated calendar where a date can be chosen.

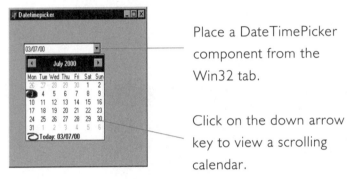

Place a DateTimePicker component from the Win32 tab.

Click on the down arrow key to view a scrolling calendar.

The DateTimePicker component has a number of useful properties. The DateFormat property allows you to choose whether the date is displayed in the long (e.g. 03 July 2000) or the short (e.g. 03/07/2000) form. The Kind property can be used to set whether the component is to be used for recording a date or recording the time.

Controlling the date type using two buttons

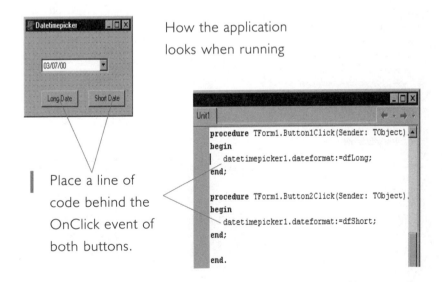

How the application looks when running

Place a line of code behind the OnClick event of both buttons.

```
procedure TForm1.Button1Click(Sender: TObject)
begin
    datetimepicker1.dateformat:=dfLong;
end;

procedure TForm1.Button2Click(Sender: TObject)
begin
    datetimepicker1.dateformat:=dfShort;
end;

end.
```

Using a Timer

A timer allows you to specify an event to be run at timed intervals set by you. The Timer component is non-visual (it disappears from view when your application is run).

The changing label program

This example shows the effect that can be created when a timer is used to amend the Caption property of a label (label1).

Amend the Interval property on the Timer component.
This property determines the interval between the OnTimer event being executed. As a guide, every value of 1000 = 1 sec.

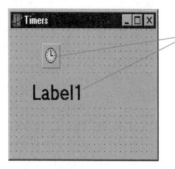

1 Place a Timer component and a Label component onto a form. Set the timer's Interval property to 5000 (5 secs).

The Tag property is found in many Delphi components.
Its purpose is defined by the programmer and as such has no particular defined meaning to the actual component where it is available.
Here, it is simply used to let the event code know whether to replace the label caption with the first or second statement.

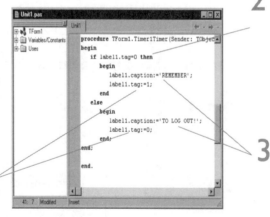

2 Double-click on the OnTimer event of the Timer component (to enter code fired at each pre-defined interval).

3 Enter code to change the Caption property of Label1.

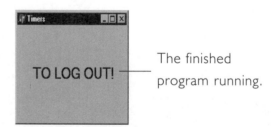

The finished program running.

Using the MediaPlayer

The MediaPlayer component allows you to play music and video through your Delphi applications.

The Internet is a great source of free WAV and MIDI music files. These two file formats are the most popular for playing music.

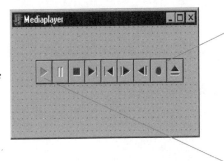

1 From the System component tab, put a MediaPlayer component on your form.

2 Set the AutoOpen property to True.

3 Select an appropriate WAV/MIDI/AVI file in the Filename property.

4 Compile and run the application. Click on the Play button.

You can also play video (AVI) using the same methods described for sound.

Adding music to your application.

When you add a MediaPlayer component you can amend its settings to hide the component, and automatically play the attached music file.

Program code held behind a form's OnShow event is executed each time the form is displayed.

```
Unit1

procedure TForm1.FormShow(S
begin
    mediaplayer1.open;
    mediaplayer1.play;
end;


end.
```

1 Open the OnShow event of the form (not the component).

2 Open the MediaPlayer component.

3 Play the file held in the Filename property of the MediaPlayer component. (To load a new file programmatically, simply add the following line of code: mediaplayer1.filename:='soundfilename.wav')

Adding an image

The Image component is used to allow you to display image files in your application. This can be useful if you are looking to incorporate a product or company logo into your design.

Adding an image component

Images can add life to your application and they are becoming the norm in terms of professional software applications.

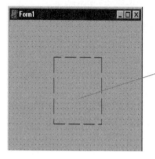

1 From the Additional component tab, add an Image component to your form.

The Image component supports all the major graphic types including BMP, GIF, JPEG, ICO and WMF file types.

2 Select the Picture property and find and load an image.

3 Click Open and then OK.

You can use a scanner or digital camera to grab images to use within your application.

4 Resize the Image component to suit the loaded image.

5 Run your application and view the added image.

Working with speed buttons

Speed buttons are buttons that can have an image displayed on them. They have special properties that make them useful for creating toolbars and differ from standard buttons as they cannot receive focus (they are not included as stop points when you tab through other form components).

Adding a speed button

1 Add a Panel component to your form and set its Alignment property to alTop.

2 Add three speed buttons to the panel. Load a suitable image into each speed button's Glyph property.

3 Set the GroupIndex property in each speed button to be the same numeric value (any value). This makes the speed buttons act as a group. Every time a button is depressed it stays down until a different button is pressed.

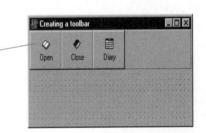

4 When your application runs, the depressed button stays down.

Using a BitBtn

The BitBtn component is a button that can display an image (a bitmap) on its face. In all other respects it is similar to a standard button.

Adding a BitBtn

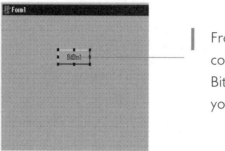

1 From the Additional component tab, place a BitBtn component on your form.

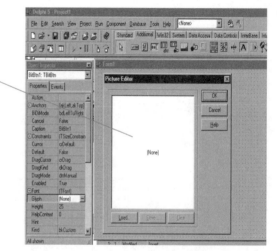

2 From the Object Inspector, choose the Glyph property and load the Picture Editor.

3 Choose an image to be loaded from your hard disc. Delphi comes pre-loaded with useful button images. Use the Windows Find utility to look for the Buttons folder and choose your image from here.

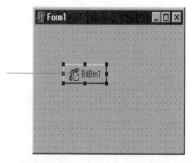

Understanding the Kind property

The BitBtn component has a very useful property called the Kind property. The Kind property provides you with a set of commonly used buttons which you can incorporate into your application with little effort.

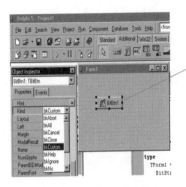

Choose the Kind property and select a button type. The bkCustom button allows you to add your own chosen glyph as previously described.

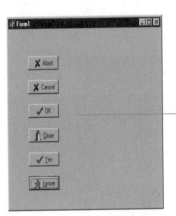

Example buttons reflecting changes made to the Kind property. Note the Glyph and Caption properties are automatically set. These buttons can also carry out preset events.

The Layout property

Change the Layout property to choose where a glyph appears on the button face.

Working with tabs

Every form has a tab order. This order determines the sequence that control will pass to components when the user presses the Tab key. It's important to set the tab order for each form as most users will choose to use the tab key rather than clicking on the mouse to move between fields.

You can disable a component's ability to have control passed to it by setting the component's TabStop property to False.

Setting the tab order

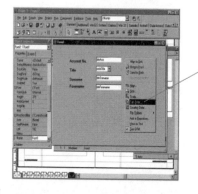

I Right-click anywhere on the form or on any component. Choose the Tab Order option.

Labels are not affected by tabs. It is unlikely that you would have any reason to pass control to a label.

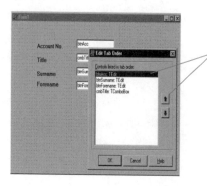

2 Highlight each component and use the arrow keys to determine the tab order for the form. The first tab stop should be placed at the top of the list.

The components on the adjacent example have had their name properties changed to a meaningful name. This is good programming practice.

Manually setting the tab order.

You can also set the tab order manually for a form by choosing each component and entering the number in the Tab Order property. The starting tab value for the first tab stop is 0. Also, if you amend a component's tab order manually, Delphi renumbers the TabOrder of the other form components.

More about properties and events

In Delphi, you can easily change similar component properties for a number of components. This saves you having to individually select and change component properties.

You can select a number of components by holding down the left mouse button and dragging over the required components.

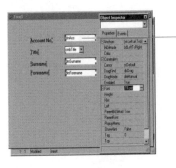

1 Select components by holding down the Shift key and clicking each component.

2 Press F11 to launch the Object Inspector. Amend the required property and the change will be reflected in all selected components.

The ActiveControl property

Every form has an ActiveControl property. This property determines which component has initial focus when the form is opened. Only one component can have focus at any one time. The following program code (placed in the form's OnShow event) is used to give the first button focus:

ActiveControl:=btnAcc

Common properties and events

The most common properties that you have come across to date are the Caption, Name, Font and Enabled properties. These properties can be found in most components and are the most common properties to change. The most common event that you've looked at to date is the OnClick event. The OnEnter and OnExit events are also commonly used. The OnShow component is also widely used to fire an event when a form is displayed. Take some time to view the properties and events for all the common components that you have used so far in this book. If you're unsure about the purpose of any of these proprieties or events, remember you can press the F1 key when the property or event is highlighted to view details of its purpose.

More about buttons

If control is sitting with another button other than the Default or Cancel buttons then the OnClick event of that button will be executed on pressing Enter or Esc. The Default and Cancel buttons only operate when control does not rest on a button.

The Default and Cancel properties

The button component has a Default and Cancel property. If the Default property is set to True, then if control is on another component and the user presses the Enter key the OnClick event of the Default button is executed. Similarly, if the user presses the Esc key, the OnClick event of the button with the Cancel property set to True will be enacted.

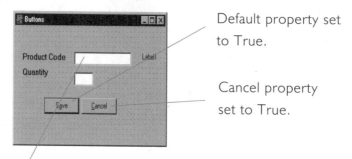

Default property set to True.

Cancel property set to True.

Only one button on each form should have the Default property set to True and only one should have the Cancel property set to True.

Press the Enter or Esc key when control is with this Edit box. The appropriate button's OnClick event will be executed.

The 'Catch the Button' example!

Place the following code behind the OnMouseOver event of a button and run the program.

Randomize and Random are built in procedures and functions of Delphi. You do not need to know how they work, you simply should know how to use them in your programs.

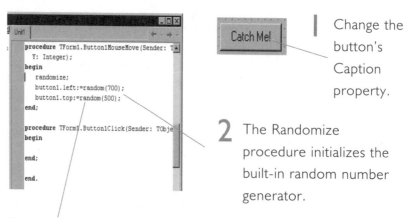

```
procedure TForm1.Button1MouseMove(Sender: T
    Y: Integer);
begin
    randomize;
    button1.left:=random(700);
    button1.top:=random(500);
end;

procedure TForm1.Button1Click(Sender: TObje
begin

end;

end.
```

Catch Me!

1 Change the button's Caption property.

2 The Randomize procedure initializes the built-in random number generator.

3 Assign a random number (between zero and the value shown) to the Left and Top properties of the button.

Creating Forms

This chapter will introduce you to working with forms in Delphi. You will find out about the different form types available as well as how to add forms to an application and add meaningful controls to each form. You will also discover some neat ways to develop and work with forms.

Covers

Chapter Three

Project forms

Each form is held as a DFM file. This file holds details of the form's size and functionality – you needn't worry about this as Delphi deals with it without any manual intervention.

In Delphi, forms are the foundations on which applications are built. Each application, whether it be a simple reporting system or a complex data entry and analysis system, will be made up of a number of forms. Each form is filled with components of many different types such as buttons, combo boxes, edit boxes and labels.

Viewing project forms

There are a number of ways of viewing forms in Delphi.

Use the Project Manager in the View menu to access forms. The project manager gives you a visual representation of how your project files interact and it also allows you to set up relationships and share files between distinct projects.

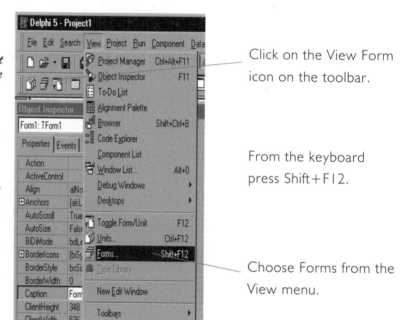

Click on the View Form icon on the toolbar.

From the keyboard press Shift+F12.

Choose Forms from the View menu.

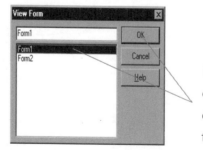

No matter which method you choose, a list of forms is displayed. Click on any form in the list to open it. Click OK.

Delphi form types

Apart from the basic Delphi form (the one that's most used) there are a number of different form types which can be used in your project.

An About form is used to allow you to display version numbers, copyright detail and contact information.

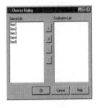

A Dual List form is used to allow you to present a number of choices and then allow the user to make a variable choice from the options listed.

A Tabbed Pages form allows you to display more than one page of components per form. This is useful if you wish to group a form into specific categories.

Three other sample forms exist and these are associated with printing data (see Chapter Six). The benefit of using the forms available in the Delphi library is that you only require to amend the properties of the components that exist on the form rather than building the form from scratch.

Choosing a pre-defined form

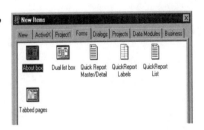

From the File menu, click New. From the New Items window, choose the Forms tab and click on the required form from the icons provided. Click OK.

Adding a form

To date, you have worked with only one single form within your Delphi projects. This is unrealistic as any applications that you build are sure to require more than one form. Forms are named sequentially from Form1 upwards.

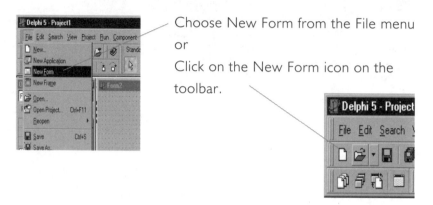

Choose New Form from the File menu

or

Click on the New Form icon on the toolbar.

You can also add a new form by choosing one of the pre-defined forms that are shipped with Delphi (described on the previous page).

The basics of a new form

When you add a form to your project, ensure that you carry out the following steps.

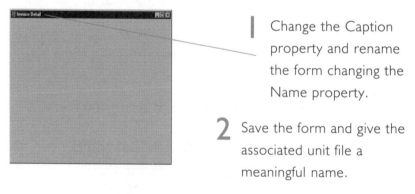

1 Change the Caption property and rename the form changing the Name property.

2 Save the form and give the associated unit file a meaningful name.

3 Set the BorderStyle and BorderIcons property for the form to suit the needs of the form. As a rule, you should set these properties to only give users access to controls they need.

Deleting a form

Sometimes you will want to remove a form from a project. This might occur if a part of your application is no longer required or if you combine the contents of multiple forms onto a tabbed pages form.

Deletion – Method 1

Removing a form from a project causes Delphi to remove all traces of the form from the Uses clause in the project's DPR file. The actual form and associated unit still exist.

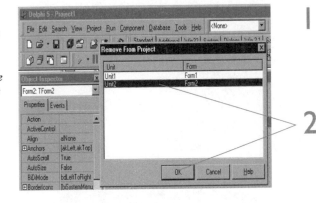

1 Click Remove From Project in the Project menu.

2 Choose the required form and click OK.

Deletion – Method 2

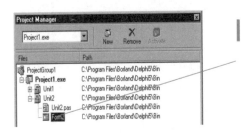

Choose the Project Manager option from the View menu. Choose and remove the required form.

When adding a form to a project the unit name appears in the Add to project dialogue box rather than the form name.

Adding an existing form to a project.

You can add an existing form to a project easily in Delphi. Forms previously removed from a project can be added this way as well as forms associated with other projects.

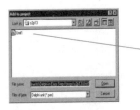

From the Project menu choose Add To Project and locate and select the required unit to be added.

Creating a splash screen

A splash screen is used to display a message to the user when your application is loading. This is particularly useful if your application is large and takes more than a few seconds to load. A typical splash screen will include the logo and version number of the application.

Set the form's BorderIcons options to False. There is no need to give the user any control in a splash screen.

1 Create a new form, name it and add some text, a panel or bevel and an image (from the Additional tab).

Adding a splash form involves amending the main project's controlling unit file. Be very careful when you are doing this as this is where the application is setup, where all forms and units are listed and where the application is initialised.

2 From the View menu, open the unit with the same name as your project.

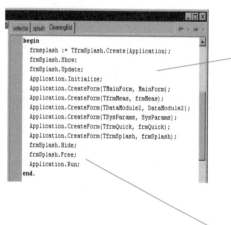

3 There are five lines of program code added to this unit relating to the splash screen (in this case named frmSplash). The first three lines after the 'begin' relate to creating the form and displaying it on the screen. The two lines near the 'end' hide the form and free memory.

There are other places in a Delphi application where a splash screen can be set up.

When you name a form, the caption of that form defaults to the value held in the Name property. Always change the Caption property independently of the Name property.

4 Check to ensure that you have made no other amendments to the existing program code otherwise your application may not compile or run.

Opening forms

As stated, 99% of your applications created using Delphi will have more than one form. Opening more than just the default form is straightforward.

Opening forms using the Show method can be a problem, especially if your screen resolution is set to a low setting. The Show method allows multiple forms to be kept opened and this can get messy and difficult to read when the display settings are low.

Place two buttons onto the main form.

Method 1

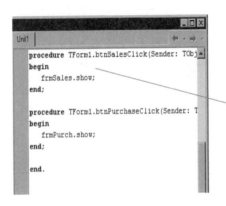

```
procedure TForm1.btnSalesClick(Sender: TObj
begin
    frmSales.show;
end;

procedure TForm1.btnPurchaseClick(Sender: T
begin
    frmPurch.show;
end;

end.
```

Add the command formname.show behind the OnClick event of each button. Make sure that you have added two new forms to your project and named them accordingly.

Method 2

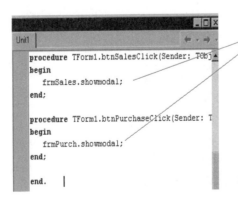

```
procedure TForm1.btnSalesClick(Sender: TObj
begin
    frmSales.showmodal;
end;

procedure TForm1.btnPurchaseClick(Sender: T
begin
    frmPurch.showmodal;
end;

end.
```

Add the command formname.showmodal behind the OnClick event of each button. This makes sure that, when users open the form, they cannot do anything outwith it until they close it.

Closing forms

A form is closed by issuing the Close method behind a button or menu, or by clicking Close from the form's system menu. The OnCloseQuery event for the form is then checked to see if the form is in a state to be closed.

The Caption property determines the text displayed on the button.
The Name property determines the actual name of the component.

Place a button onto your form. Change the Caption and Name properties.

2 In the OnClick event of the button, call the Close method.

3 At the moment you do not know what type of code would normally be placed in the OnCloseQuery event. However, this is a useful place to carry out some final checks (e.g. whether data on the form has been changed) or carry out some final validation before the form is closed.

Remember

Users can also close a form by clicking on the system menu and choosing Close.

Even when the user closes the form using the system menu, the form's OnCloseQuery event is still run allowing you to make final checks before closing the form.

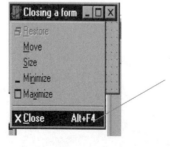

Click on the system menu of the form and choose Close. Alternatively, press Alt+F4.

Common form properties and events

Like all Delphi components, a form has specific properties and events that are regularly used by system designers.

Common properties

 Don't worry when you look at the many properties of a form. Only a few common properties are used regularly – the rest can simply be left with the values that they hold by default.

 Add a file in the form's Image property and select an image to be displayed when the form is minimised or displayed.

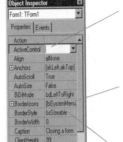

Choose the component to receive focus when the form is displayed.

Choose which menus will appear on the form when the application is run.

Allows you to set rules for the form's border.

Determines the default font for the form. All components added to the form will default to this font type.

 In Delphi, you should note that form events are run in the following order:

1. *OnCreate*
2. *OnShow, and;*
3. *OnActivate*

Determines the screen position of the form when it is displayed.

Common events

The OnActivate event occurs when the form receives focus.

The OnCreate event is run when the form is created.

The OnShow event is run when the form is shown.

The program code that you write to make your form perform a particular task will be placed behind the form's events. Practice will let you know which events to use for particular tasks.

Changing the form sequence

Your Delphi project will manage the forms in it in the order that they were added to the project. In most situations this will be fine, as you will design your application from the first form down. However, you may have cause to change the main form to load a different form when the application is run.

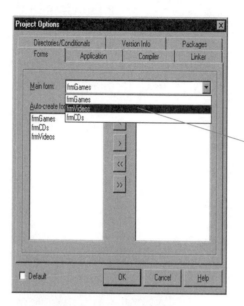

1 From the Project menu, choose Options.

2 In the Project Options window, click the main form field and replace the selected form with another form shown in the list.

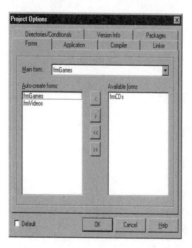

3 You can also remove a form from the Auto-create forms list. Simply highlight the form and choose the > button. The form will move from the Auto-create forms list to the Available forms list. When you do this, the removed form will no longer operate if it is called within your application.

A tabbed pages form

The standard form available in Delphi is the most commonly used. However, you can use a tabbed pages form to allow you to display information that would normally take up more than one form screen. A tabbed pages form allows you to split your form with a number of pages – each page giving access to the complete surface area of the form.

Tabbed pages on a form are useful where the information displayed is related but would normally take up more than one screen. A good example is personal information that might be contained in a personnel system.

1 From the File, New menu option, click on the Forms tab and choose the Tabbed Pages icon.

Before changing the tab page name, remember to click on the main form area under each tab.

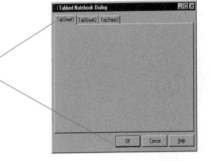

2 The blank form displayed comes with three buttons and three tabbed pages.

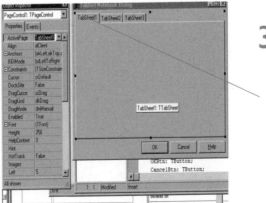

3 Click on each tab and, in the Object Inspector, change the Caption property to something more meaningful.

4 You can now place components on any of the tabbed pages.

Skill and practice will ensure that you select the right area in a tabbed page form before changing properties in the Object Inspector – it can be quite confusing!

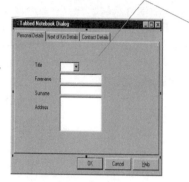

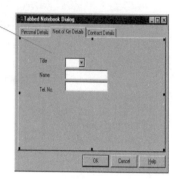

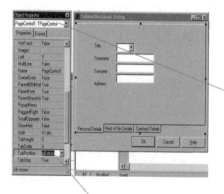

5 Click in the area surrounding the page tabs and choose the PageControl's Object Inspector.

6 Change the TabPosition property to amend the position of the tabs on the form.

7 To add a new tabbed page to the form, right-click in one of the current tabs and choose New Page. You can also delete a tabbed page from the same menu.

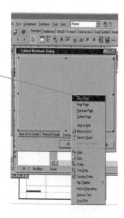

Basic Programming Skills

In this chapter you will learn some of the basics of good programming. You'll find out about variables, constants and the control loops that underlie all computer programs. You will also learn about functions in Delphi, arrays and how to print your forms and units. Finally, you'll learn a bit about event driven programming principles.

Covers

Chapter Four

Using numeric variables

Variables are specific areas of memory that are used to store data that you are working with in your application. Variables can be thought of as 'temporary pigeon holes' where data can be stored and changed. In Delphi, variables can be 'declared' in a unit or within specific procedures such as the OnClick event of a button.

Numeric variables

Numeric variables store integer and real numbers.

The Adding Machine example

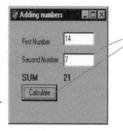

The user can enter two integer numbers, press the Calculate button and the sum of the two numbers will be displayed.

Enter the following program code behind the OnClick event of the 'Calculate' button.

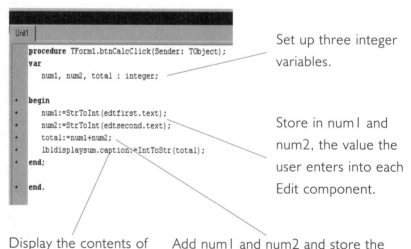

```
procedure TForm1.btnCalcClick(Sender: TObject);
var
    num1, num2, total : integer;

begin
    num1:=StrToInt(edtfirst.text);
    num2:=StrToInt(edtsecond.text);
    total:=num1+num2;
    lbldisplaysum.caption:=IntToStr(total);
end;

end.
```

Set up three integer variables.

Store in num1 and num2, the value the user enters into each Edit component.

Display the contents of total on the screen.

Add num1 and num2 and store the result in the variable total.

Real Number variables

Real number variables are used when you are working with decimal numbers. In newer versions of Delphi, recommendations are that you use the Double data type as opposed to Real.

StrToFloat is used to covert string variables to float (real) values.
FloatToStr fulfils the opposite function.

The Adding Machine example (using real numbers)

Here, the second number entered by the user is of type real.

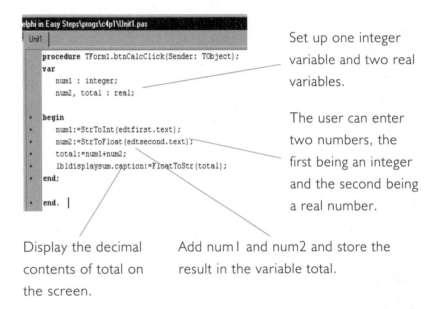

```
elphi in Easy Steps\progs\c4p1\Unit1.pas
Unit1
procedure TForm1.btnCalcClick(Sender: TObject);
var
    num1 : integer;
    num2, total : real;

begin
    num1:=StrToInt(edtfirst.text);
    num2:=StrToFloat(edtsecond.text);
    total:=num1+num2;
    lbldisplaysum.caption:=FloatToStr(total);
end;

end.
```

Set up one integer variable and two real variables.

The user can enter two numbers, the first being an integer and the second being a real number.

Display the decimal contents of total on the screen.

Add num1 and num2 and store the result in the variable total.

Declaring variables

In the above example all variables are declared in the 'var' section of the procedure. To declare a single variable or more than one variable of the same type, list each variable in a comma separated list. Follow the variable list with a colon (:) and then declare the variable type. Finish each declaration with a semicolon(;).

```
var
    rate : real;
    age : integer;
```

The DIV operator

The DIV operator is used for integer division. It takes two integer numbers, divides one by the other and displays only the whole number part of the answer, discarding the remainder.

Using the DIV operator, 20 divided by 3 would give an answer of 6 (Three into eighteen goes 6 times, remainder 2).

The Change from a Pound Example

In this example, the DIV operator is used to work out the coinage required for change of any monetary value below £1.

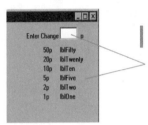

In the example shown, the variable 'change' is recalculated after each coin has been determined. This must be carried out to reduce the value yet to be calculated for the remaining coinage denominations.

1 Add an Edit component and 12 Label components detailing the coinage below £1 – name these labels.

2 Place this program code behind the Edit component's OnChange event.

3 Set up a variable for each coin and set these variables to zero. Include a variable for the xhange value entered.

Between steps 3-4, do the following. For each coin, use the DIV operator to determine the number of coins of that denomination that will be included in the change. Repeat this for all coins (only some shown in program code).

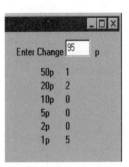

4 Run the application and see the coinage breakdown for the change value entered.

The MOD operator

The MOD operator is also used for integer division. It takes two integer numbers, divides one by the other and displays only the remainder part of the answer, discarding the whole number part.

Using the MOD operator, 20 divided by 3 would give an answer of 2 (Three into eighteen goes 6 times, remainder 2).

The Machine Wastage example

In this example, the MOD operator is used to work out the wastage when a sheet of metal is cut into equal sized parts.

1   Add two Edit and associated Label components detailing the size of the sheet of metal and the lengths to be cut (include a label to display wastage).

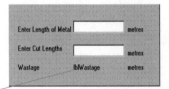

2   Place this program code behind the second Edit component's OnExit event.

3   Declare three suitably named variables.

```
nit1.pas
Jnit1

procedure TForm1.edtCutLengthExit(Sender: TObject);
var
    totlength,cutlength,wastage:integer;

begin
    totlength:=StrToInt(edtTotalLength.text);
    cutlength:=StrToInt(edtCutLength.text);
    wastage:=totlength mod cutlength;
    lblWastage.caption:=IntToStr(wastage);
end;

end.
```

4   Convert to integer and store the values that the user enters into the Edit components.

5   Use the MOD operator to determine the wastage when the metal has been cut.

6   Run the application and see the wastage value displayed.

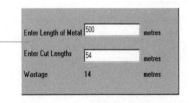

Basic structure of program code

Delphi uses Object Pascal. This requires you to follow certain rules when writing program code. If you do not follow these rules, various syntax errors will occur when you compile your applications.

Statements and expressions

A statement in Object Pascal looks something like:

Each statement in your program code should be terminated with a semicolon (;).

wage:=hrswrked*rate;

All Delphi code is written as a number of statements. Here, the variable 'wage' takes the value of the result when 'hrswrked' is multiplied by 'rate'. Just to confuse things, this statement is made up of an expression. An expression is a piece of code that has some sort of a calculation (in this case hrswrked*rate). Variables can also appear in expressions:

wage:=wage+bonus;

Arithmetic operators

When you write Delphi code you will undoubtedly use the common arithmetic operators: * / + and -. If you are working with complex expressions then normal arithmetic rules apply.

wage:=wage+othrs*otrate; (othrs is multiplied by otrate and the result added to wage)

In a simple expression, the calculation is carried out left to right.

wage:=wage+bonus+otpayment;

The Assignment Operator(:=)

Replace the value held in the variable to the left of the assignment operator with the result of the expression on the right.

Other variable types

If you declare a fixed length string variable then the size of the variable *represents the maximum number of characters that you can store in it.*

Apart from working with numbers, you are likely to work with both string and logical variables as you develop applications in Delphi.

String variables

String variables are used to store text.

```
procedure TForm1.btnPressClick(Sender: TObjec
var
    streetname:string;
    postcode:string[8];
begin
    streetname:='High Street';
    postcode:='CA3 1RS';
end;

end.
```

1 Declare two variables, one fixed length.

2 Assign two values, each in single quotes, to the two variables.

The ShowMessage function displays the message in quotes and presents the user with an OK button. This function is discussed later in this book.

To declare a variable that simply holds one character such as A,B,C,a,b,c you should use the data type, CHAR.

Boolean variables

Boolean variables can hold only one of two values at any point in time – True or False.

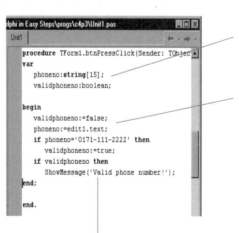

```
elphi in Easy Steps\progs\c4p3\Unit1.pas
Unit1
procedure TForm1.btnPressClick(Sender: TObjec
var
    phoneno:string[15];
    validphoneno:boolean;

begin
    validphoneno:=false;
    phoneno:=edit1.text;
    if phoneno='0171-111-2222' then
        validphoneno:=true;
    if validphoneno then
        ShowMessage('Valid phone number!');
end;

end.
```

1 Declare two variables, make one Boolean.

2 Set the initial value of 'validphoneno' to False.

3 Assign the phone number entered into the Edit component by the user into the string variable, 'phoneno'.

4 Verify if the phone number entered matches the one listed. If it does, display an appropriate message to alert the user.

Constants

Constants are variables that have a particular value assigned to them in a procedure or unit. Constants cannot change value when your application is running and can be used as many times as required throughout a procedure or unit.

Currency Convertor example

You cannot assign values to constants at run-time.

Constants are great for large applications where you can use a value on many occasions throughout the code. If the value the constant represents changes (e.g. VAT rate) then you only need to change the value in the Const area and the change will be made throughout the application.

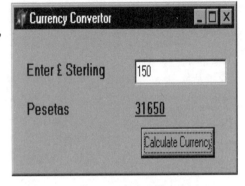

This example will allow you to convert pounds(£) to pesetas.

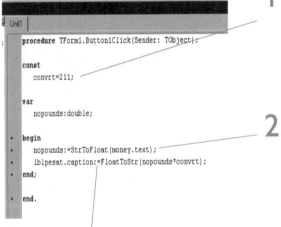

1 Declare the constant in the Const area of your event procedure.

2 Read the value the user enters in the Edit component.

3 Calculate the converted value and display it in the Caption property of a label.

There is no requirement to declare the type of a constant (e.g. Real, Integer). When you declare each constant, the correct type is automatically associated with that constant.

Repeating your program code

In Delphi, there are number of ways to execute a piece of program code one or more times. These statements are known as control structures as they affect how your application operates. The following examples show the three most common repetitive control structures.

The FOR statement can start at a value other than one e.g. for kount:=5 to 9 do.

The FOR statement

The FOR statement allows you to repeat a statement or group of statements on a specified number of occasions. This statement can be used to count either upwards from a low value or downwards from a high value.

Use the FOR statement with the downto syntax, to decrement a number. E.g. for kount:=10 downto 1 do.

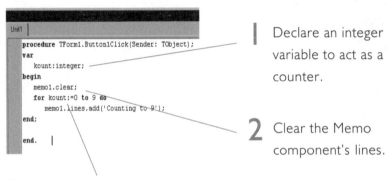

```
Unit1
procedure TForm1.Button1Click(Sender: TObject);
var
    kount:integer;
begin
    memo1.clear;
    for kount:=0 to 9 do
        memo1.lines.add('Counting to 9');
end;

end.
```

| Declare an integer variable to act as a counter.

2 Clear the Memo component's lines.

3 Starting at 0, add a line of text to the memo component until the value of kount is equal to 9.

The While statement

The WHILE statement is used to execute a number of lines of program code until a condition is evaluated as True. The WHILE statement will continue to run if the condition is evaluated as False.

A SpinEdit component is found on the Samples tab page and allows you to grab an integer value by clicking the arrows on the component. The value is stored in the Value property.

The Multiplication example

Drop two SpinEdit components and a Memo component onto a form. Set the SpinEdits Maxvalue and Minvalue property to suitable values.

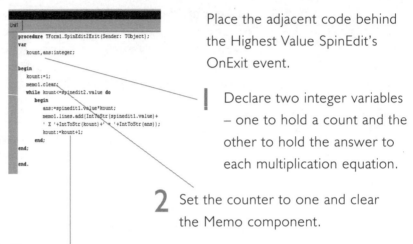

Place the adjacent code behind the Highest Value SpinEdit's OnExit event.

1 Declare two integer variables – one to hold a count and the other to hold the answer to each multiplication equation.

When assigning more than one value to a text property such as edit.text or memo.lines, you can use the + key to join each component part to be added.

2 Set the counter to one and clear the Memo component.

3 For each occurrence of the equation, work out the answer to the multiplication and add this to the Memo component. Increment the counter (kount) by one.

The REPEAT statement

The REPEAT statement is similar to the WHILE statement, however the code is carried out at least once.

Counting capital Es!

1 Place the following program code behind a button. Make sure that you replace component names with those chosen.

The code between 'repeat' and 'until' is carried out until you reach the end of the word entered.

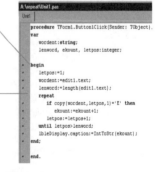

Selection statements

A selection statement is used to make a decision in program code. The decision taken will determine how the program will continue and what further statements will be executed.

To add items to a combo box, type them into the Items property of the ComboBox component.

The IF statement

The IF statement is the most common selection statement you will come across. The following example shows two versions of the statement, the basic IF statement and the IF...ELSE statement.

The Health Club example

When using the IF...ELSE statement, a semicolon cannot appear at the end of the last statement before the word ELSE as this would have the effect of terminating the IF statement at this point.

In this example, appropriate messages will be displayed depending on the membership grade displayed in the combo box.

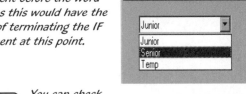

Add this program code behind the OnChange event of the ComboBox component (combobox1).

You can check expressions using any of the following operators:

< (less than)

> (greater than)

= (equal to)

<> (not equal to)

<= (less than or equal to)

>= (greater than or equal to)

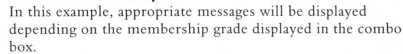

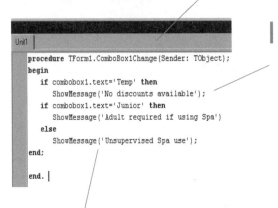

```
Unit1
procedure TForm1.ComboBox1Change(Sender: TObject);
begin
    if combobox1.text='Temp' then
        ShowMessage('No discounts available');
    if combobox1.text='Junior' then
        ShowMessage('Adult required if using Spa')
    else
        ShowMessage('Unsupervised Spa use');
end;

end. |
```

| In this statement the expression is evaluated. If it's true (the grade is 'temp') the message is displayed; if not, no message appears.

When an expression is evaluated in an IF statement the result is Boolean – it's either True or False.

2 In this version of the IF statement, if the member is 'Junior' then the first message is displayed, if the membership grade is anything else (no matter what) the second message is displayed instead.

The CASE statement

The CASE statement might be described as being a glorified IF statement. In essence, it is an IF statement that allows you to make a choice from a number of options.

The CASE statement will only work with ordinal values. An ordinal value is a distinct value that has an obvious, distinct and definitive pattern. Example, 1,2,3 or A, B, C. The CASE statement does not work with real numbers.

The Exam Grade example

In this example, you can choose a grade from a combo box and display a message dependent on the grade chosen.

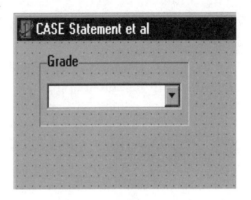

Choose a grade and display an appropriate message.

| Add a ComboBox component to your form and any associated formatting components.

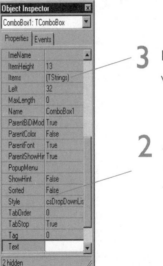

3 In the Items property, place the values 1,2,3,4,5 in the list.

2 Amend the Style property to csDropDownList. This ensures that you cannot type a rogue entry by mistake when making a choice from the combo box.

4 Place the listed program code behind the OnChange event of the combo box. This will ensure that the program code is executed if the user makes a new choice from the list.

If the chosen value is found, the statement after the colon is executed.

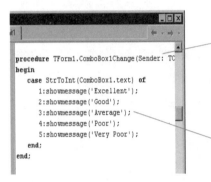

Convert the text value from the ComboBox component to an integer value.

List the values that your grade can have, each followed by a colon.

Adding an ELSE clause

It is good practice to include an ELSE clause in a CASE statement. This clause acts as a catch all and returns a value if the user enters a value outwith those in the main CASE statement.

If the user enters a number outwith the range 1 to 5, then the ELSE clause is executed and the message displayed.

The CASE statement running.

User defined data types

Most of the variables you use in Delphi will be set up as one of the standard types such as integer, real, double, string or Boolean. However, it can be useful to create your own user-defined data types – or enumerated types. The following program code shows a simple example of using user-defined data types.

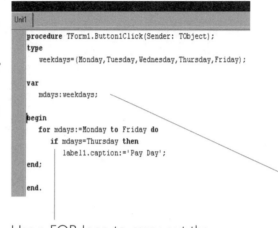

```
procedure TForm1.Button1Click(Sender: TObject);
type
    weekdays=(Monday,Tuesday,Wednesday,Thursday,Friday);

var
    mdays:weekdays;

begin
    for mdays:=Monday to Friday do
        if mdays=Thursday then
            label1.caption:='Pay Day';
end;

end.
```

Set up a type called weekdays and list the entries valid for this type – the days of the week.

Declare a variable of the new type, so you can manipulate data via the user-defined type.

Use a FOR loop to carry out the assignment statement to the label. This loop will be repeated five times – representing Monday to Friday.

Two other functions can be used with enumerated types:

Pred
The Pred function allows you to determine the previous entry in the enumerated list.

Pred(Tuesday) – will return Monday.

Succ
The Succ function will return the next entry in the enumerated list.

Succ(Tuesday) – will return Wednesday.

String functions

You can also join two strings using the '+' sign e.g. edit1.text+edit2. text.

The UpperCase function converts a string to upper case letters.

A function is a piece of code that is written once and which can be called to carry out a specific program task whenever needed. Delphi provides you with libraries of useful functions.

String functions

String functions allow you to manipulate string data. These functions are particularly useful where you are looking to manipulate numeric data gathered from, for example, an Edit component. Here, the data entered is stored as a string variable (in the Text property of the Edit component) and therefore requires conversion to a numeric (integer or real) before further calculation can be done. The following functions are amongst those most commonly used:

NOTE: All examples use edit1.text='ABCDEFGH' , edit2.text='346', edit3.text='45.43'

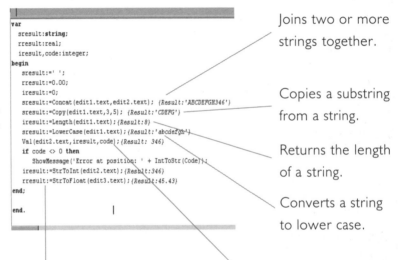

```
var
  sresult:string;
  rresult:real;
  iresult,code:integer;
begin
  sresult:=' ';
  rresult:=0.00;
  iresult:=0;
  sresult:=Concat(edit1.text,edit2.text); {Result:'ABCDEFGH346'}
  sresult:=Copy(edit1.text,3,5); {Result:'CDEFG'}
  iresult:=Length(edit1.text);{Result:8}
  sresult:=LowerCase(edit1.text);{Result:'abcdefgh'}
  Val(edit2.text,iresult,code);{Result: 346}
  if code <> 0 then
      ShowMessage('Error at position: ' + IntToStr(Code));
  iresult:=StrToInt(edit2.text);{Result:346}
  rresult:=StrToFloat(edit3.text);{Result:45.43}
end;

end.
```

Joins two or more strings together.

Copies a substring from a string.

Returns the length of a string.

Converts a string to lower case.

Converts a string to either an integer or a real number.

Converts a string to a numeric variable which is listed after the string variable(iresult). If code has a value other than 0 then the string doesn't exclusively contain numerals. Use the IF statement to identify the position of the problem in the string and trap the error.

Numeric functions

Numeric functions

Numeric functions work on numeric data such as integers and real numbers. These functions allow you to manipulate numbers within your Delphi applications. The most popular functions are discussed below.

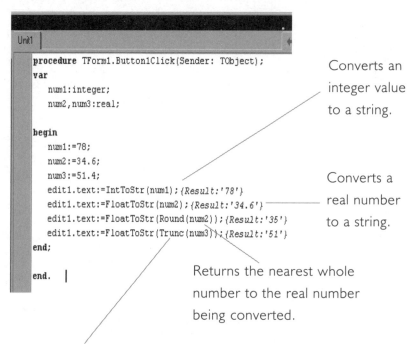

```
procedure TForm1.Button1Click(Sender: TObject);
var
    num1:integer;
    num2,num3:real;

begin
    num1:=78;
    num2:=34.6;
    num3:=51.4;
    edit1.text:=IntToStr(num1); {Result:'78'}
    edit1.text:=FloatToStr(num2); {Result:'34.6'}
    edit1.text:=FloatToStr(Round(num2)); {Result:'35'}
    edit1.text:=FloatToStr(Trunc(num3)); {Result:'51'}
end;

end.    |
```

Converts an integer value to a string.

Converts a real number to a string.

Returns the nearest whole number to the real number being converted.

Functions have rules regarding what can be done with them. You must follow these rules otherwise you will get errors when you try to compile your project.

Returns the integer portion only of the real number being converted.

Functions within functions

Delphi allows you to include functions within other functions. This is an essential tool that is used extensively when building applications.

FloatToStr(Round(num2))

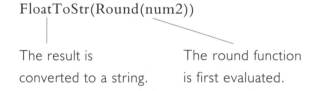

The result is converted to a string.

The round function is first evaluated.

Arrays

The array listed is a one dimensional, or '1-d', array. More complex grid like array types exist for complex calculations.

An array is a group of variables that have a similar name but operate independently. Arrays can be set up to store and manipulate data in a similar fashion to any standard variable. An array is declared in the Var section of a unit or procedure.

```
var
    weekday:array[1..7] of real;
```

The above declaration sets up an array which contains seven elements:

weekday[1], weekday[2] through to weekday[7]

Weekly average rainfall example

In the rainfall example, the code listed should be placed behind the OnExit event of the edit component associated with Sunday's rainfall. When the user presses the tab key to leave this reading, the average rainfall will be displayed.

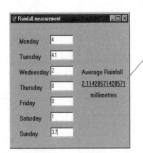

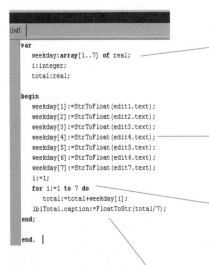

Declare a real array with seven elements (weekday) a counter (i) and a running total (total).

Assign the contents of each of the 7 edit components on the form to the array elements.

Use a FOR statement to read through the array, adding the values held into a running total value.

Assign the average rainfall (total/7) to a label's caption property which is displayed on the form.

To align the Labels and Edit components quickly, select a group of components, right-click and choose Align.

Printing

When you're working with your Delphi project there will be times when you want to print your forms and program code. This is essential for showing customers, desk-checking your logic and completing program documentation.

Printing a form

It is a good idea to regularly print project forms and units. This gives you a record of older versions of the software should your computer crash or should you notice a programming problem at a later date.

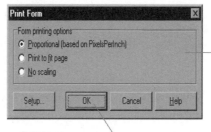

Open a form and choose Print from the File menu. The Print Form dialogue box is shown.

2 Choose the option required for your print. Forms can be printed proportionally, expanded to fit the printed page, or printed as they appear. Click OK.

Printing a unit

To print a selected range of a large unit, select the range and click on the Print selected block check box.

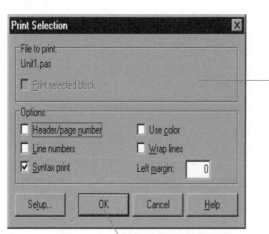

Open a unit and choose Print from the File menu. The Print Selection dialogue box is shown.

2 Use the check boxes to print the unit with line numbers against each line of code, with page numbers, with long lines wrapped onto the next line and with color print. Click OK.

Using Database Tables

In this chapter you'll find out how to create and use a database in Delphi. You will learn how to add database tables to forms and view and navigate through records. You'll also find out how to add, edit and delete data as well as find out how to search for specific data.

Covers

Chapter Five

A database – the basics explained

A database is a collection of related tables that allow you to record and manipulate data. Databases are very flexible and are used by professional programmers to create both simple and complex applications. A database can be sorted into any order and data can be filtered to show only certain information.

Delphi can easily use existing databases created using commercial packages such as DBaseIV, Oracle, Paradox and Microsoft Access.

Table

A database table is a collection of records and fields that relate to a specific purpose e.g. customer table, employee table, video film rental table.

Video film rental table

Table fields

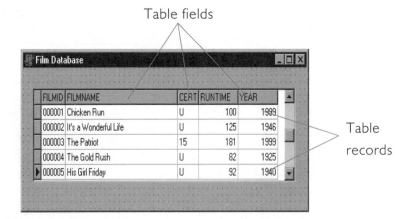

FILMID	FILMNAME	CERT	RUNTIME	YEAR
000001	Chicken Run	U	100	1999
000002	It's a Wonderful Life	U	125	1946
000003	The Patriot	15	181	1999
000004	The Gold Rush	U	82	1925
000005	His Girl Friday	U	92	1940

Table records

Records

Each record (row) in a table lists information about a specific transaction such as a particular employee or a certain video film. Each table will have a number of records dependent on the application being built.

Fields

Each field (column) in a table relates to a specific data item such as an employee surname, age or the certificate of a particular video film. Each field has a name which is shown at the top of each column and this field name is generally set up to be a specific size and type.

The Database Desktop

The Database Desktop is a database tool that allows you to create and structure database tables. You can edit data from the Database Desktop and you can work with tables created in Paradox, dBASE, and SQL formats.

In this book you'll use the Database Desktop to create and manipulate tables.

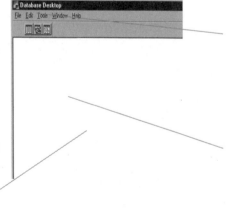

To launch the Database Desktop choose it from the Tools menu.

Every time you open a table in Database Desktop, it will appear in its own window.

The menu options allow you to open database tables as well as sort data and add/edit data.

The Database Desktop window appears after you launch Database Desktop. Here, you can manage tables and create and run queries (discussed later).

When you open a database table, the data records are displayed here.

Opening an existing table

Try opening an existing database table and viewing the contents of the table.

From the File menu, choose the Open menu item then locate and open your table.

Creating a table

The following example creates some basic fields in an employee table. This table will then be available for use in your Delphi applications.

Examples in this book use dBase for Windows tables. If you choose to create different table types remember to follow the field naming and field type rules of that particular database application.

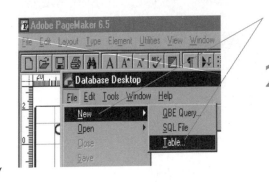

1 From the File menu choose New, Table.

2 Choose dBase for Windows as the table type.

To insert a new field between two existing fields, simply highlight one of the fields and press Ins. A new field is created above the existing field. To delete a filed, highlight it and press Ctrl+Del.

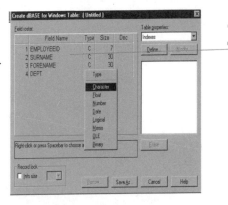

3 Add new fields to the table. For each field choose an appropriate name, field type and size. To move between each entry, use the Tab key.

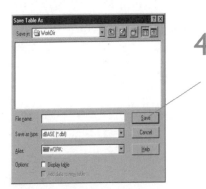

4 Give the new table an appropriate filename, choose a folder in which to store it, and click Save.

Adding an index

An index allows you to sort your table in a particular fashion. By simply choosing a field, you can then display your data and search for particular records using the chosen indexed field.

Use Table, Info Structure to simply view the structure of your table.

Open an existing table and choose Restructure from the Table menu.

Each table can have more than one index defined.

Ensure that no-one is using a database table before you commence any
indexing activity.

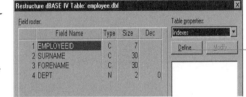

2 From the Table Properties field, choose Indexes. Click on the Define button.

Ensure that the Maintained check box is ticked. This ensures that
your index will still operate even if data in your table has been added, amended or deleted.

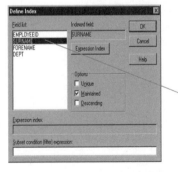

3 Highlight your chosen field and see it displayed in the Indexed field box. Click OK.

4 Give the index a suitable name and click OK.

Creating an expression index

An expression index allows you to create an index with more than one field. This ensures, for example, that a Surname+Forename index would sort a table by surname first, and within surname by forename:

Index files are held separately from actual table files. This means that you can safely delete an index file and recreate it without fear of losing any data.

Harris, John
Harris, Rita
Mills, Frank
Mills, Harry

I Open an existing table and choose Restructure from the Table menu.

2 Click on the Expression Index button. Open the Define Index window.

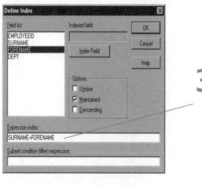

3 Click on each field to become part of your expression index. Place the + sign between each field.

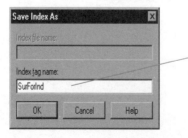

4 Give the index a suitable name and click OK.

Modifying a table structure

A table's structure is determined by its fields and their properties. You can use the Restructure Table dialogue box to change a number of table elements.

When using Paradox tables, further restructuring options are available for each table.

You must only restructure a table when you are the sole user. If your application is running on a network, make sure everyone shuts the application down before carrying out a restructure.

1 From the Table menu, choose Restructure.

2 Choose the appropriate element to change.

When you delete records from a database table they are simply marked for deletion. Packing the table physically removes them.

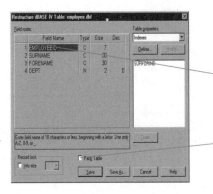

To add a field, tab to the line after the last field and type new field details.

Pack the table to remove any deleted records.

To delete a field, select it, and then press Ctrl+Del.

To change the type of the field, right click on Type and choose a new data type.

Saving your table under a different name is a good way of allowing you to check that your amendments work before overwriting your live table.

Choose the Save option to make the changes to the table structure permanent.

Choose the Save As option to save the changes to the table structure in a copy of the original table.

Setting up a BDE alias

All versions of Delphi come with BDE drivers for Paradox and dBase. The client/server version comes with a wide variety of drivers including Oracle and Sybase.

Before you can add a table to your forms you must set up an alias. Delphi comes shipped with the Borland Database Engine (BDE). The BDE enables access to a wide variety of database products. The BDE acts as a middle man between your application and your database.

Creating an alias

The first thing to do is to create an alias (a set of parameters that shows the name, path and type of database being used).

Set up a new alias for each new application you build (providing one doesn't exist for tables being used).

1 Launch the BDE Administrator program from the Delphi group.

2 In the Object menu, choose New.

3 Choose the Standard driver type. Click OK.

If you distribute your application to different PCs, you must setup the same alias on each PC you load the application on.

4 Name your new alias and press Enter.

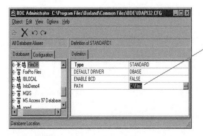

5 Choose the correct driver for your database and then set the path to point to the folder containing your tables. That's it – a new alias created. Close the BDE.

Adding a table to a form

Now that you have successfully created database tables and set up a BDE alias, the next thing you will want to do is to add a table to a form.

1 From the Data Access component tab, drop a Table component onto your form.

Delphi provides a standard set of aliases. You will see these when you add a table to your form. These aliases and associated tables are useful for practice.

2 Choose the database alias from the drop down list in the DatabaseName property of the table component.

3 Choose your table from the drop down list next to the TableName property.

4 If you created an index file for your table using the Database Desktop, then choose it from the IndexFieldName property drop down list.

5 Give your table an appropriate name.

Adding a DataSource component

Once you've added a Table component you need some way of linking this dataset to the components that you'll use to navigate and display your table data. A DataSource component provides this interface.

Each table that you use on your form requires a data source if you wish to view and manipulate the data.

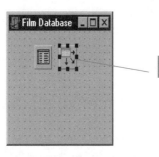

| From the Data Controls tab, choose and place a DataSource component.

2 To link the data table to the Table component already placed on the form, you must choose the table name from the Dataset property. Your table is now ready to be used.

If a component is 'data aware' this means that it can be used to link to a database table and perform a function on that data.

Once you have added a DataSet and a DataSource component, you can choose data-aware components from the Data Controls tab to allow you to present and manipulate the data contained in your table.

Viewing your table with DBGrid

The DBGrid component, found on the Data Controls tab, allows you to display your table data in spreadsheet format.

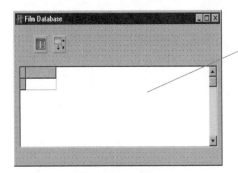

Place a DBGrid component on a form containing a Table component and associated DataSource component.

 The Table and DataSource components are not visible on your form when your application is run.

2 Click on the DBGrid component and Open the Object Inspector.

 The DBGrid component has a number of useful properties that add appeal and professionalism to your application. Take a look at Options and TitleFont.

3 Choose the data source name from the drop down list against the DataSource property. This links the DBGrid to your data.

 Right click on the DBGrid and choose the Column Editor. This allows you to add/remove columns to be shown in the grid. Note: the removal of columns does not effect the underlying data.

4 Click on the Table component and change the Active property to True.

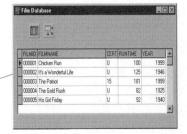

Your data should now be displayed.

Adding navigation keys

The DBNavigator component allows you to link your DBGrid to buttons that will allow you to navigate through your data as well as add, edit and delete records.

Use the Tips property within DBNavigator to add user-defined tips for the buttons on the navigator bar. Remember to set the ShowHint property to True.

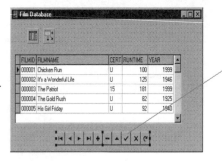

1 Place a DBNavigator component on the form.

2 Hook the DBNavigator up to your data source by linking to the required DataSource component in the DataSource property.

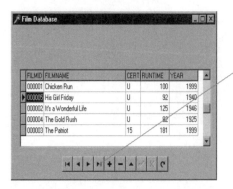

3 Run your application. You can now use the navigational keys to move forward and backwards through your table data.

Simple data manipulation

The DBNavigator component provides powerful buttons that allow you to add, edit and delete data from your table as well as traverse through your table.

Direct editing of the DBGrid has the same effect as using the edit keys on the navigator bar.

Be careful when editing data on the DBGrid. Ensure that you do not overwrite important data by mistake. Pressing the down/up arrow key to move to another record, posts any changes back to the database.

Go to next record.   Go to last record.   Delete a record.   Save changes.   Cancel changes.

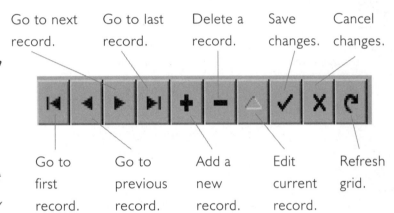

Go to first record.   Go to previous record.   Add a new record.   Edit current record.   Refresh grid.

Determine which buttons are visible on the navigator bar by changing their settings in the Visible Buttons property.

Changing the Options property of the DBGrid component allows you to set rules for users so they will be unable to directly enter data into the grid. Rather they will have to use edit screens set up by the application developer. This is useful when you simply wish to view table data.

Set dgEditing to False to disable grid data entry.

Set dgRowSelect to True to highlight the current record.

Searching

Searching through your database table allows you to quickly locate records. This is especially useful in large databases.

When using FindKey you must ensure that the correct index file is chosen. If more than one index file exists, choose the one that matches the field to be searched on.

Place an Edit component and a Button component onto your form. When the button is pressed, the search routine will be performed.

Searching using FindKey

If no record is found in step 2 when using FindKey, display a message.

FindKey is used to search a database table where an index file exists.

If an index file exists, Locate will attempt to use it when searching. This speeds up the search process.

1 Set the IndexName property of the Table component of the table to be searched.

2 Use FindKey (behind the OnClick event) to find the value entered in the edit box.

Searching using Locate

To locate a field irrespective of case, include loCaseInsensitive in the FindOptions parameters (separate each option with a comma).

Searching using Locate doesn't need the table to be indexed.

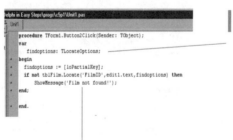

In step 2 when using Locate, the loPartialKey parameter instructs the search to find the first match, even on incomplete film IDs.

1 Define a variable of type TLocateOptions. This specifies the values in the Options parameter of the Locate method. LoPartialKey allows you to search on the first few characters of the film id.

2 Locate the first record that has a FilmID of the value held in edit1.text.

Writing Reports

In this chapter, you'll find out how to write reports using QuickReport, a report generator that comes with Delphi. As well as defining basic reports, you'll discover how to add groups and footers; do calculations; and include only certain subsets of data in your final report.

Covers

Chapter Six

Using QuickReport

QuickReport is an excellent, flexible tool that can be used to build reports for inclusion in your Delphi application.

Earlier versions of Delphi used a less sophisticated reporting tool known as ReportSmith.

Creating a sample report

This report uses the sample file 'animals.dbf' provided by Delphi in the DBDEMOS database.

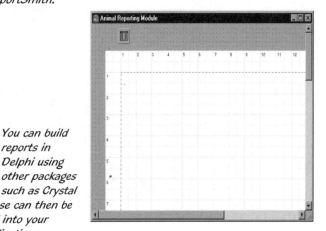

Place a Table and DataSource component on your form. Link these to a database table.

You can build reports in Delphi using other packages such as Crystal Reports. These can then be incorporated into your finished applications.

QuickRep component.

2 From the QReport component tab, place a QuickRep component on the form. This component acts as the base on which your report will be constructed.

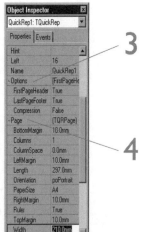

3 Change the Options property to determine how headers and footers will print.

4 Change the Page property to determine margin size, paper orientation and paper size.

Creating a basic template

Before you add data to your report, first you must set the correct report layout. The following bands are common to all reports created using QuickReport.

1 Place a QRBand component onto your QuickRep component. It will automatically place itself and default to a Title band.

A QRBand.

2 Add a QRLabel component, and change its Caption property to 'Animal Report 01'.

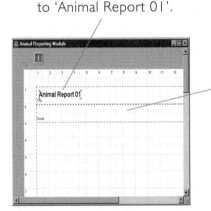

3 Add another QRBand component. This time change its BandType property to rbDetail.

4 Add another QRBand component. This time change its BandType property to rbColumnHeader.

5 Add any other QRBands you deem appropriate (rbPageHeader, rbPageFooter etc.).

Adding table data

The QuickRep component, QRLabel and QRText components must all link to the data table on the form. To do this, choose the table from the drop down DataSet list on each component. Your report will not work if you omit this step.

Ensure that the Active property of your table is set to True before previewing your report. If it is set to False, no data will be displayed.

Adding data to a QuickReport simply requires the use of two further components – the QRLabel and QRText components.

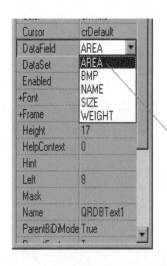

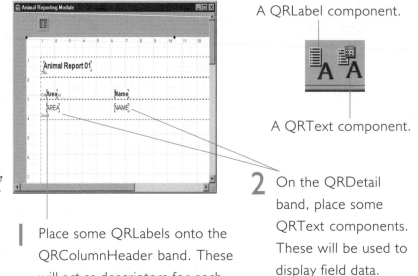

A QRLabel component.

A QRText component.

1 Place some QRLabels onto the QRColumnHeader band. These will act as descriptors for each report column.

2 On the QRDetail band, place some QRText components. These will be used to display field data.

Associating table data with a QRText component

Cursor	crDefault
DataField	AREA
DataSet	AREA
Enabled	BMP
+Font	NAME
+Frame	SIZE
	WEIGHT
Height	17
HelpContext	0
Hint	
Left	8
Mask	
Name	QRDBText1
ParentBiDiMode	True

1 Click on a QRText component in the QRDetail band. Press F11 to launch the Object Inspector.

2 Associate the QRText field with a table and a field within that table by amending the DataSet and DataField properties.

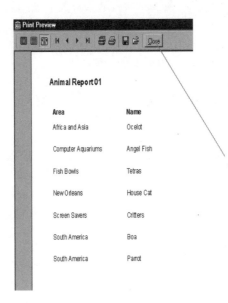

3 Preview your report by right-clicking and choosing Preview from anywhere within the QuickRep band.

4 Click on Close to return to the Delphi desktop.

The menu icons at the top of the Print Preview window provide you with a number of useful reporting utilities.

Saving a report to disk is useful if you need to keep a history of reports at particular points in time.

You can save your report to disk and load the saved report (with data) at a later stage.

Print Setup lets you change your printer.

Print will print the previewed report.

Zoom to Fit allows you to view your report as it will look when printed.

100% shows how the report will look in its actual size.

Zoom to Width fits the report on your screen.

Navigational keys to move through report pages.

Adding a group

A group can be added to your report to allow a split in the data to be included. The following example splits the animals into area groupings.

When working with QuickReport bands it's easy to become confused. Always remember what action you last performed to allow easy backtracking.

Add a QRGroup band to your report. Open the Object Inspector for this group and link the Master property to the main QuickRep component. The QRGroup component will automatically reposition itself on the report.

2 Choose the Expression property of the QRGroup component and click on the Database field button.

Removing the AREA field from the rbDetail band after adding a group simply avoids repetition when you print your report.

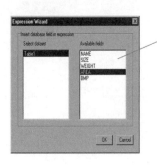

3 Choose the default dataset and then choose the Area field to group on geographical area. Click OK.

4 Add a suitable QRLabel to the QRGroup band and remove the AREA field from the rbDetail band and place it in the QRGroup band.

...cont'd

You can tighten your printed report by reducing the spacing available in each band. This is done by simply moving components and reducing the size of the band by dragging its handles.

5 Preview your grouped report.

Adding a goup footer

A group footer allows you to place a band that will appear under each group. This might, for example, include some summary of the group data.

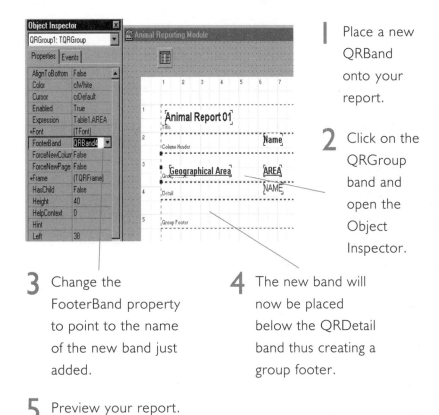

1 Place a new QRBand onto your report.

2 Click on the QRGroup band and open the Object Inspector.

3 Change the FooterBand property to point to the name of the new band just added.

4 The new band will now be placed below the QRDetail band thus creating a group footer.

5 Preview your report.

Adding other bands

Each QuickReport created can include a number of bands. Two other useful bands are the rbPageFooter and rbSummary bands.

Adding a page footer

 The bottom right hand corner of each band includes a label detailing which type of band is displayed.

An rbPageFooter band will display its content at the bottom of each printed page.

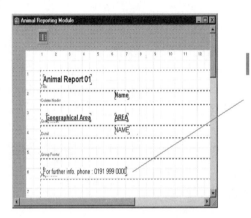

Add a QRBand to your report and change its BandType to rbPageFooter. Add a suitable QRLabel component.

Adding a summary

A summary band will be printed after all group and detail bands.

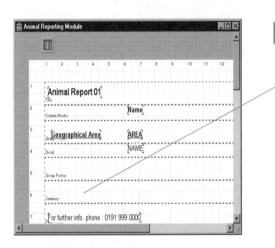

Add a QRBand to your report and change its BandType to rbSummary. This summary band will be used to display overall summary information for the report.

Performing calculations

Whilst QuickReport is excellent for printing table field data there will undoubtedly be a need to create reports that carry out some sort of calculation. QuickReport provides a useful component to help.

Using the QRExpr component

You'll now add a count of the animals in each group to your report as well as an overall animal count.

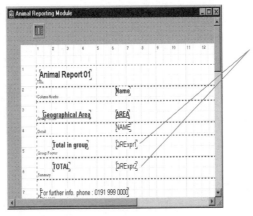

1 Add a QRExpr component to the group footer and summary bands.

2 Add suitable descriptive QRLabels.

3 Click on the QRExpr component in the group footer band. Click on the Expression property and open the Expression Wizard.

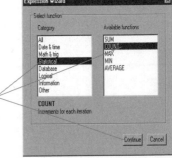

4 Click the Function button. From the Statistical category, choose COUNT. Click Continue.

If you wanted to perform a calculation on the animal count, add another QRExpr component to the group footer field. Then, in the Expression Wizard enter, for example:

count*4.70

This might work out the average daily cost to feed the animals in each group.

5 Click OK.

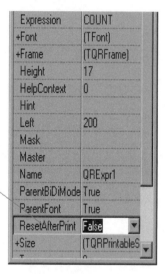

6 Open the Object Inspector for the QRExpr band in the group footer area. Change the ResetAfterPrint property to True. This will ensure that the count resets itself after each geographical group.

Once you become confident, you can key the functions you require straight into the Expression Wizard for each QRExpr component.

When displayed, expressions may have inconsistent decimal points. To fix this, place 0.00 in the Mask property of the QRExpr component.

7 Repeat the exact same steps listed above, only this time select the QRExpr component on the report summary band.

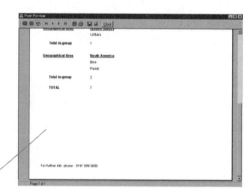

8 Preview your report.

Filtering data

Sometimes when you print a report, you will only want to include a subset of your data rather than include the complete table data.

You must ensure that the filter expression entered conforms to the rules of the database environment that you are using for your tables.

Filtering at design-time

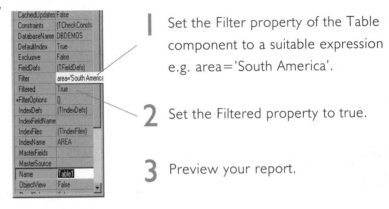

1 Set the Filter property of the Table component to a suitable expression e.g. area='South America'.

2 Set the Filtered property to true.

3 Preview your report.

Filtering data at run-time

You can also filter data programmatically when your application runs.

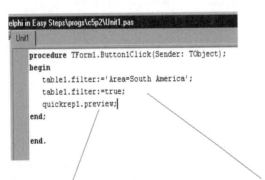

```
elphi in Easy Steps\progs\c5p2\Unit1.pas

Unit1

procedure TForm1.Button1Click(Sender: TObject);
begin
    table1.filter:='Area=South America';
    table1.filter:=true;
    quickrep1.preview;
end;

end.
```

You can print your report direct in the program code by calling the reportname.print.

1 Add a button to your form.

2 Place the adjacent code behind the OnClick event of the button.

This will preview your report automatically on pressing the button.

These lines of code assign the expression that determines the data to be included in the report.

3 Run your application. Press the button and see a preview of your filtered report.

Formatting your report

By now you will be familiar with the creation of a QuickReport using a mixture of bands and components. However, these reports are basic when viewed. You can enhance your final report by the addition of a number of useful components and activities.

Change the Font property of each component to add interest to your report.

Adding the date, time and page number

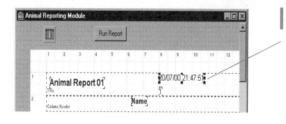

| Add two QRSysData components to the title band of your report.

To align your components, select a group of components, right-click and align as required.

2 In the top QRSysData component, change the Data property to qrsDateTime. Change the second component to qrsPageNumber.

3 Add a QRImage component to add a rectangle to your title. Size accordingly, then right-click and send the image to the back.

A formatted report preview

Advanced Database Use

In this chapter we'll look at using database tables for more advanced uses. You'll discover how to add special table fields as well as how to validate data ensuring that minimum errors occur at run-time. You'll also look at working with tables in different states, and learn how to filter your data to include only specific table details. You will also find out how to create a master-detail relationship and, finally, you'll look at using the Database Form Wizard to make creating database tables a breeze.

Covers

Chapter Seven

Adding a calculated field

A calculated field is a field added to a database table that performs a calculation as you move from record to record. The values held in a calculated field are not permanent.

Adding a Calculated field to 'stock.dbf'

Here, you will add a calculated field to multiply the quantity of each item with the unit price giving a stock value.

The Fields Editor allows you to select from the table only those fields to be included in the dataset being used.

You can open the Fields Editor by simply double-clicking on a Table component.

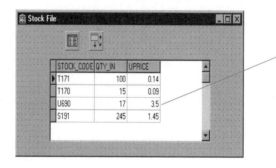

1 Create a stock table, add data and place it on a form. Add a Table and DataSource component and link the data to the grid (DBGrid component).

2 Open the table's Fields Editor. (Right-click on the table component, choose Fields Editor).

3 Right-click and choose Add all fields.

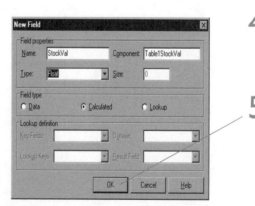

4 Right-click in the Fields Editor and choose New field.

5 Give the calculated field a meaningful name and define its data type. Click OK.

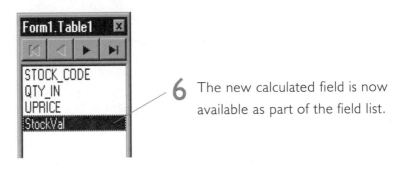

6 The new calculated field is now available as part of the field list.

The OnCalcFields event for a table runs regularly – checking and updating any of the table's calculated field values.

Calculating the value for the Calculated field

Now that you've created a calculated field you must make it execute a calculation.

I Select the Table component. Launch the Object Inspector and double-click in the OnCalcFields event.

Always set the ReadOnly property of the calculated field to True. This will prevent users accidentally overwriting the calculated value. You can do this from the Fields Editor.

```
\Unit2.pas
Jnit2

procedure TForm2.Table1CalcFields(DataSet: TDataSet);
begin
    Table1stockval.value:=Table1qty.value*Table1uprice.value;
end;
```

2 Include the calculation to determine the stock value.

3 Compile and run your application. Note the calculated field shown.

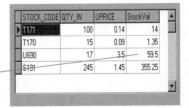

STOCK_CODE	QTY_IN	UPRICE	StockVal
T171	100	0.14	14
T170	15	0.09	1.35
U690	17	3.5	59.5
S191	245	1.45	355.25

Adding a Lookup field

A lookup field is a read-only field that allows you to display the result of a search. This search is often used to supply description fields from other tables for tables holding coded items such as a stock table.

Adding a stock description from a separate table

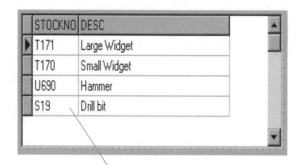

1 Add a new Table component to your form. In the example shown, the table holds stock code and description values.

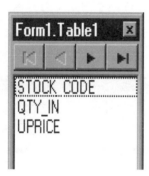

2 Open the original table's Fields Editor (the table containing stock codes, quantities and values). Right-click the Table component, then choose Fields Editor.

3 Right-click in the Fields Editor and choose New field.

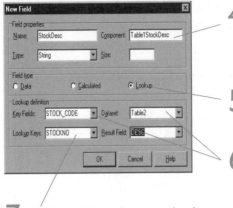

4 Add a suitable name and field type for the lookup field.

5 Choose Lookup.

Amend the DisplayLabel property in the Object Inspector for each field to create a more formatted heading for the field when displayed in a grid.

6 Choose the key field to be used to search for the stock description. Choose the dataset to be searched.

7 In the table being searched, identify the field to be used and the field to be displayed if a match is found.

8 Compile and run your application. Note the lookup field shown.

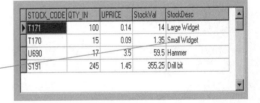

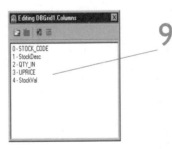

9 Click on the DBGrid's Column property to open the Columns Editor. Drag the StockDesc column to the second entry in the list.

10 The finished view.

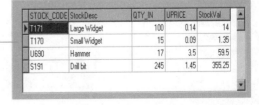

Validating data-aware components

To date, the examples you have created have not included any real data validation. Validating data allows you to trap errors made by users when using your application.

Data-aware components

The common data-aware components you will use have similar components in the Standard and Advanced tabs – although these components don't link directly to a dataset.

In the last chapter, when you added field data onto your QuickReport, you first came across data-aware components. Data-aware components are available in Delphi to let you work with data – these are found in the Data Controls tab.

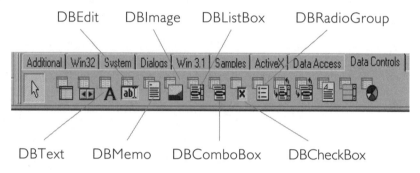

DBEdit   DBImage   DBListBox   DBRadioGroup

DBText   DBMemo   DBComboBox   DBCheckBox

You must have a DataSource component available to your form to use data-aware components.

Hooking up a data-aware component

All data-aware components require to be associated with a specific table field.

Data-aware components work with real data. Make sure you practice on a demo database table first.

1 In the DataField property of the component (a DBEdit here), choose the field to be linked to the component.

The data displayed in data-aware components reflects that of the current record in the database table that the component is hooked up to.

2 Link to a data source.

3 Scroll down and change the MaxLength property to the maximum field size for this component.

Testing for a blank field

To view your data table fields properties and events through the Object Inspector, make sure that you Add all field in the Fields Editor of each table component that you place on your form.

One of the most common activities you will do is check for a blank field. This ensures that, for example, a mandatory field like a surname is always complete when the user is entering data.

The OnSetText event

This event is very useful for managing data entry in a data-aware Edit component. It is automatically run when you type a new value into the Edit component.

1 Add a DBEdit component to your form and link it to a data field.

2 Select a field in the Object Inspector (in this case LastName).

3 Click on the Events tab and select the OnSetText event.

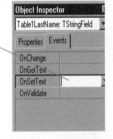

The abort method stops the current process.

4 Add the adjacent code which will display a message if the field is blank and return the user to the field to re-enter a non-blank value.

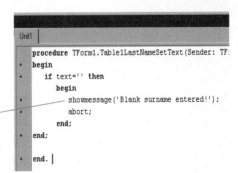

```
Unit1

procedure TForm1.Table1LastNameSetText(Sender: TF:
begin
  if text='' then
    begin
      showmessage('Blank surname entered!');
      abort;
    end;
end;

end. |
```

Exception handling

When working with components and functions you can implement exception handling to help ensure that your application runs error free. Functions and components raise exceptions when something goes wrong – you might think of these as alarm bells, alerting the programmer to take corrective action.

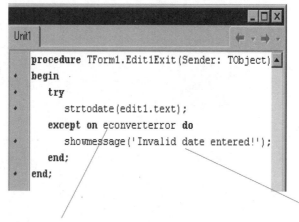

If an error is detected in any lines of program code (there can be more than one) between the 'try' and 'except' then program control jumps to the error handler code after the 'except on...' and this is then carried out. You could say that the program code between the 'try' and 'except on' is protected.

Checking for an incorrect date

In this example, a date entered into a simple Edit component is checked for correctness.

```
procedure TForm1.Edit1Exit(Sender: TObject)
begin
   try
      strtodate(edit1.text);
   except on econverterror do
      showmessage('Invalid date entered!');
   end;
end;
```

The function is carried out (on the OnExit event of the edit1.text component).

An EConvertError is raised if an error is detected in the line(s) of code after the 'try'. Here, the function StrToDate raises the exception if the value entered into the edit1.text component is not in the recognised standard date format.

A suitable message is displayed alerting the user to the mistake.

An EConvertError is raised when a line of code in your application tries unsuccessfully to convert a float, integer, date or time value to a string value or vice versa. It is also raised if you try to use a conversion function on an incorrect value – in the example shown above.

Dividing by zero

The EDivByZero exception is raised when an application attempts to divide an integer value by zero. The EZeroDivide exception is raised when an attempt is made to divide a float value (such as a real variable) by zero.

There are a number of different exceptions that can be raised. The ones discussed are some of the more common ones used.

EDivßyZero

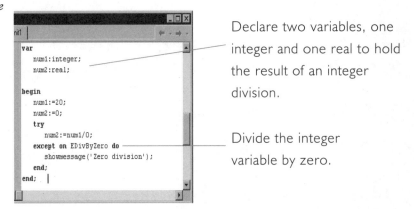

Declare two variables, one integer and one real to hold the result of an integer division.

Divide the integer variable by zero.

If an exception is raised then carry out the code after the 'except...on'.

EZeroDivide

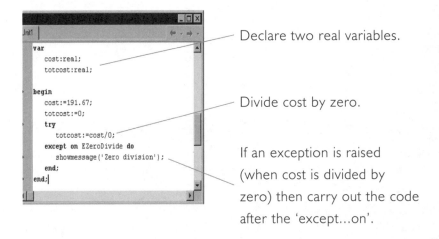

Declare two real variables.

Divide cost by zero.

If an exception is raised (when cost is divided by zero) then carry out the code after the 'except...on'.

Filtering a table

When you work with data tables you generally work with a subset of a table rather than the whole table. For example, in a customer table, you might be interested only in those customers who live in a certain geographical area or in an employee table you might only want to work with employees who fall above a certain salary scale. We have previously looked at amending a table's Filter property – we will now look at filtering data using the Table component's OnFilterRecord event.

Before any table filter will take effect you must ensure that the table's Filtered property is set to True.

Employees' earnings example

In this example, the grid displays only those employees earning over £40,000.

This example uses the employee table in the DBDEMOS database.

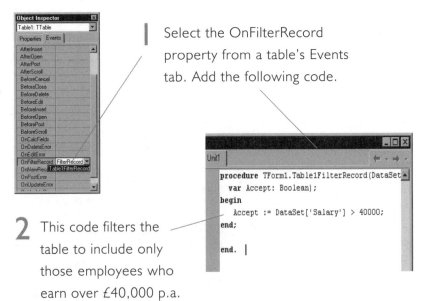

1 Select the OnFilterRecord property from a table's Events tab. Add the following code.

```
procedure TForm1.Table1FilterRecord(DataSet
  var Accept: Boolean);
begin
  Accept := DataSet['Salary'] > 40000;
end;

end.
```

2 This code filters the table to include only those employees who earn over £40,000 p.a.

3 View the filtered table data in a grid.

Table state

A table's state determines the current status of the table when the application is running. This value will change dependent on what your application is actually doing. The most common states are Browse, Edit and Insert mode.

Browse mode

This is the default mode when a table is opened for use (its Active property is set to True). In Browse mode the table data can be viewed but cannot be amended in any way.

Closing a data form

The following code, placed behind a form's OnCloseQuery event, will alert you to a table that is not in Browse mode and thus should maybe be saved before leaving the form.

> **|** Check to determine if the table is in a mode other than Browse.

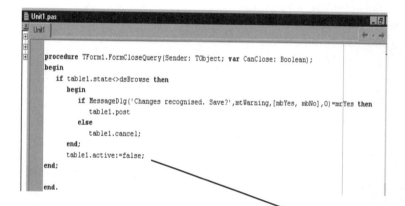

```
Unit1.pas
Unit1

procedure TForm1.FormCloseQuery(Sender: TObject; var CanClose: Boolean);
begin
    if table1.state<>dsBrowse then
        begin
            if MessageDlg('Changes recognised. Save?',mtWarning,[mbYes, mbNo],0)=mrYes then
                table1.post
            else
                table1.cancel;
        end;
        table1.active:=false;
    end;

end.
```

2 Display a message to the user (this particular type of message allows a response to be made.)

3 If the user decides to save the current record, then post it to the database otherwise cancel the changes and close the form.

Edit mode

If a table is in Edit mode then the data contained in each record can be amended.

Checking to see if a table is already in Edit mode

The following code, placed behind a simple button, checks to see if a table is in Edit mode. Suitable messages are displayed.

```
Unit1.pas
Unit1

procedure TForm1.Button3Click(Sender: TObject);
begin
    if table1.state<>dsEdit then
        showmessage('Unable to edit.')
    else
        showmessage('Ready to edit.');
end;
```

Insert mode

If a table is in Insert mode then new records can be added to the table.

Adding a record to a table

The following code, placed behind a simple button, checks to see if a table is in Insert mode.

To place a table into Edit mode, issue the following command:

'tablename.Edit'.

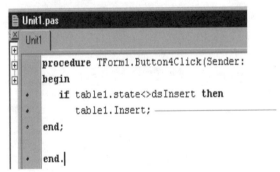

```
Unit1.pas
Unit1

procedure TForm1.Button4Click(Sender:
begin
    if table1.state<>dsInsert then
        table1.Insert;
end;

end.
```

This line of code inserts a blank record into a table and places the table in Insert mode.

Creating a master-detail relationship

Master-detail relationships allow you to link two tables with a common data field. For example, a recipe is made up of many ingredient items. When you view a particular recipe you should be able to view its component ingredient items.

Viewing recipe details

Where two tables are linked with a common field these are often known as '1-many' relationships (one to many).

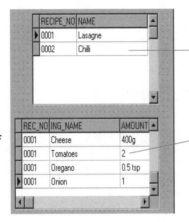

Create two database tables. One should contain recipe name details and should simply include a code and a description. The second table will contain the ingredients for each recipe – each ingredient will be a separate database table record.

Throughout this book you will come across examples where components have default names; and examples where meaningful names have been used. When you are programming in live situations, meaningful names will help you better understand the purpose of each component and variable.

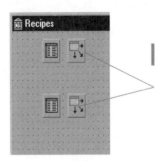

Place two Table components and two DataSource components onto a form. Link each table to a data source.

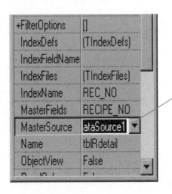

2 Link the MasterSource data source property of the ingredients table to point to the data source of the recipe name table.

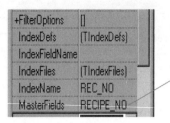

3 Click on the MasterFields property to launch the Field Link Designer.

4 Choose the index field that represents the field that links the two tables.

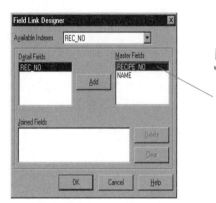

5 Highlight the two fields (one from each table) that will create the link (in this case the recipe number fields). Click the Add button followed by the OK button.

6 Place and hook up two DBGrids, one to each data source. Set the Active properties of both Table components to True. You can now click any record in the top grid and see the associated ingredients displayed only for that recipe in the bottom grid.

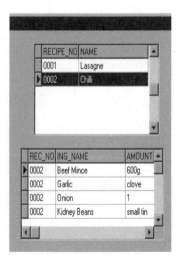

Using the Database Form Wizard

The Database Form Wizard can be used to take all the leg work out of building data-aware forms.

The employee database example

In this example you will use the Form Wizard to create a form which can be used to edit, browse or add employee details.

Use the BDE Administrator utility found in the Delphi group to create new alias names.

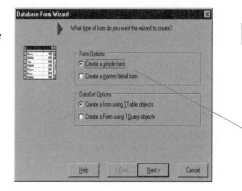

I From the Database menu, choose Form Wizard. The Database Form Wizard dialogue window will appear. From here, choose to create a simple form.

2 Click on the Next button.

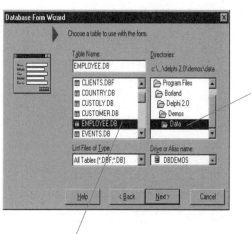

3 Either choose the path where your table is held, or choose the appropriate alias.

4 Select the table to be used in your form. Click on the Next button.

You still require to add some buttons for closing and cancelling your form.

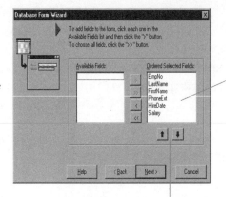

5 Click on the available table fields and either choose them all, or selectively make choices.

6 Use the arrow keys to move the fields into your desired order. Click on the Next button.

If you make changes to a record you must write these changes back to the data table. This is done by issuing the command 'tablename.post'.

7 Decide on how the fields should look on the form. Click on the Next button.

The Form Wizard creates the form with default labels and component names. Take some time to amend each component name and caption to suit your specific application's needs.

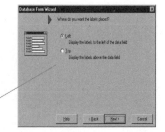

8 Decide on how labels should align with form fields. Click the Next button.

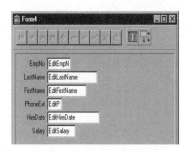

9 Generate the form. All the fields chosen from the data table are displayed with associated labels and a navigator bar to facilitate control over the table.

Querying Database Tables

In this chapter we take a brief look at SQL. You will find out how to create a simple query as well as extend your knowledge of SQL to generate query tables for particular hard-coded values or dynamic values passed to the SQL statements. You will also look at creating a query that gathers data that is incomplete.

Covers

Chapter Eight

Introducing SQL

Structured Query Language, or SQL, provides you with a great tool to easily analyse and retrieve data from relational database tables. You can also use SQL to create and manage database tables; however this book does not cover this topic. SQL originated in the 1970's when it was invented by IBM. SQL quickly gained popularity as it is relatively easy to understand for the purposes of data extraction and thus can be used as easily by less technical users such as accountants and marketing staff as well as by system developers and programmers.

Whilst SQL is relatively easy to understand it is comprehensive and is made up of many commands. This chapter gives a brief overview of the main data extraction commands.

A basic extraction

In this example, the SQL statement simply extracts all records from the employee table.

You must enter the SQL statements as they are written. If you make a mistake, an error will be displayed.

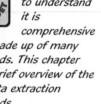
1 From the Data Access tab, place a Query component onto your form.

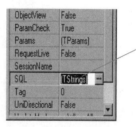
2 Launch the Object Inspector for the Query component. Select the SQL property.

When linking to a DBGrid, treat an SQL component as a Table component. Simply link it to a data source and then link the grid to the data source to see the results of the SQL extraction displayed.

3 Enter the SQL statements into the property. 'Select *' retrieves all records – 'from employee' ensures that the table used to select the data is the employee table (held in the DBDEMOS database). Click OK.

You must set the SQL component's Active property to True before you will be able to view any data.

4 View the complete extracted table data via a grid (DBGrid).

EmpNo	LastName	FirstName	PhoneExt	H
2	Nelson	Roberto	250	2
4	Young	Bruce	233	2
5	Lambert	Kim	22	0
8	Johnson	Leslie	410	0
9	Forest	Phil	229	1

Creating a basic query

SQL is very useful when you wish to retrieve data from more than one table.

Extracting stock detail

In this example, you extract stock codes from one table and match them with corresponding descriptions in another.

1 From the Data Access tab, place a Query component onto your form.

2 From the query component's Object Inspector, choose the SQL property. Add the following SQL statements. Click OK.

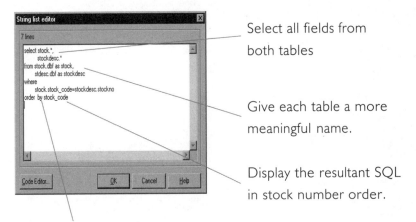

Select all fields from both tables

Give each table a more meaningful name.

Display the resultant SQL in stock number order.

Only include records where the stock_code field in the first table is equal to the stockno field in the second table.

STOCK_CODE	QTY_IN	UPRICE	STOCKNO	DESC
S191	245	1.45	S191	Drill bit
T170	15	0.09	T170	Small Widget
T171	100	0.14	T171	Large Widget
U690	17	3.5	U690	Hammer

3 View the results.

Creating a query with specific values

A more complex query allows you to include only those records in the resultant retrieval that meet a specific value.

Finding stock code T171

1 From the Data Access tab, place a Query component onto your form.

2 Launch the Object Inspector for the Query component, choose the SQL property. Add the following SQL statements. Click OK.

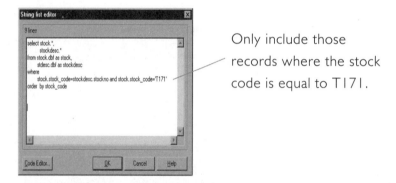

Only include those records where the stock code is equal to T171.

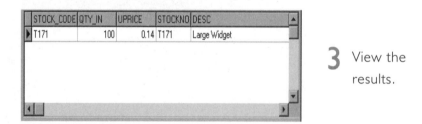

3 View the results.

Viewing selected fields

You may only want to include certain fields in your query. To do this, instead of issuing the select * command, you include a list of the field names to be included in the output.

```
select stock_code, qty_in from stock
where stock_code='T171';
```

Creating a query with dynamic values

In the previous example you created a query that included only a specific field value. Now, you'll learn how to create a query that allows the user to enter a value from an Edit component and then have this passed to the SQL to run and extract the relevant records.

Finding a user-entered stock code

1 From the Data Access tab, place a Query component onto your form.

2 Launch the Query component's Object Inspector, choose the SQL property. Add the following SQL statements. Click OK.

Only include those records where the stock code is equal to :mcode (a passed value).

3 Add a basic Button to your form and an Edit component. When the button is pressed the SQL will take the value entered by the user in the Edit component.

This code sets the query to False, then passes the value in edit1.text to the mcode parameter. The Query component's Active property is set to True and the query is run.

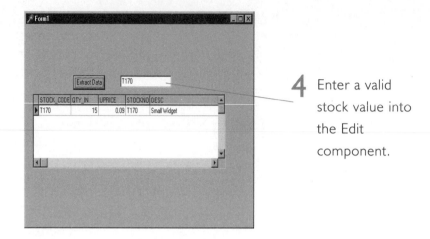

4 Enter a valid stock value into the Edit component.

5 Click on the button to run the code behind the OnClick event. The data is extracted.

Understanding parameters

In the above example the following line is the one that makes the code dynamic and more functional than a basic SQL statement:

stock.stock_code=stockdesc.stockno and
stock.stock_code=:mcode

In the above statement, 'mcode' is a variable that takes the values passed to it in the statement within the OnClick event of the button:

query3.ParamByName('mcode').AsString:=Edit1.text;

'ParamByName' is used at run-time. This means that the parameter's value in the SQL component is changed and the resultant query is run each time the component's value is amended.

Great Extras

This chapter will introduce you to some extra features, including menus, which will really enhance your Delphi applications.

Covers

Chapter Nine

Adding a toolbar

Adding a toolbar to your form allows you to create a uniform method of displaying and managing form buttons.

 You can align the toolbar with any part of your form. To do this, amend the Align property of the ToolBar component.

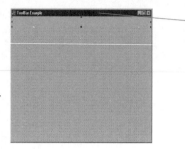

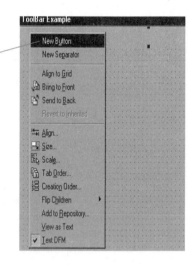

1 From the Win32 tab add a Toolbar component. This immediately aligns with the top of your form.

2 Add a new button to the toolbar by choosing the New Button menu item. Repeat this step to add a second and third button.

 You can move buttons and separators on a toolbar by simply highlighting them and dragging them to the desired position in the toolbar.

3 Add a new separator to the toolbar. This can be used to split groups of buttons into logical groups.

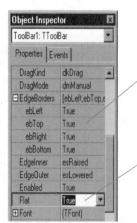

 Spend a few minutes looking at other properties on the toolbar that can be amended to suit your application's requirements.

4 Show the toolbar's border by changing the EdgeBorders properties to True.

5 Change the Flat property to True to make the toolbar appear transparent on the form.

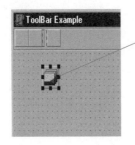

An image added to a button is known as a glyph.

6 From the Win32 tab, add an ImageList component. This will allow you to add images to your toolbar buttons.

7 Right-click the ImageList component and choose the ImageList Editor.

Button images can be found in the images\buttons directory of Delphi (this may be different for each version.)

8 Choose an image to be displayed on each button (starting from the left-most button).

When you choose an image, the ImageList Editor asks should the image be separated. Say yes, then delete the second (black and white) image from the Images list.

9 Each image displayed relates to each button on the toolbar – image 0 is the left-most button. Click OK when you have added three buttons.

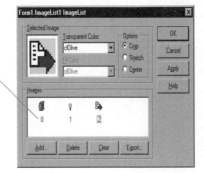

Each button on the toolbar acts as a normal button and can have events added as required.

10 Choose the Image property on the Toolbar component and link it to the ImageList component. Your images are now displayed.

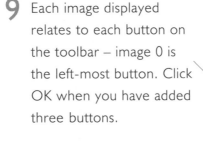

The toolbar at run-time.

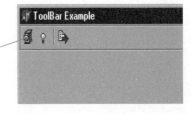

Changing the cursor

Different components will have different cursor defaults.

Each form has a Cursor property associated with it. The value of this property is normally crDefault which ensures that the cursor for the form is the type laid down by Delphi (the most common cursor type is a pointing arrow.) However, you can override the default cursor and choose a different one to be displayed.

My application is busy!

In this example, when you press the button (and launch the OnClick event), the application goes off and carries out some processing that will take longer than a few seconds. During this time you can display the hourglass cursor to alert the user that an operation is being carried out.

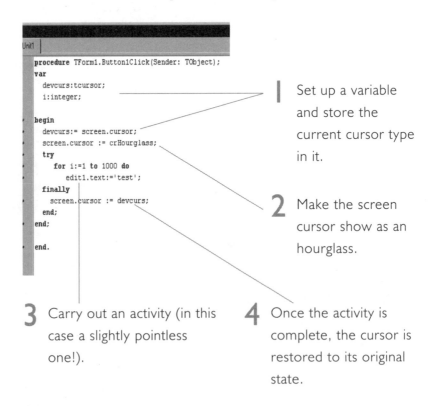

```
Unit1

procedure TForm1.Button1Click(Sender: TObject);
var
   devcurs:tcursor;
   i:integer;

begin
   devcurs:= screen.cursor;
   screen.cursor := crHourglass;
   try
      for i:=1 to 1000 do
         edit1.text:='test';
   finally
      screen.cursor := devcurs;
   end;
end;

end.
```

1 Set up a variable and store the current cursor type in it.

2 Make the screen cursor show as an hourglass.

3 Carry out an activity (in this case a slightly pointless one!).

4 Once the activity is complete, the cursor is restored to its original state.

The 'screen.cursor' refers to the screen variable which is Windows dependent.

Adding a progress bar

A progress bar allows you to let your users know how long a process is likely to take. It normally shows a percentage value and is extremely useful when starting your application.

Check back to Chapter Three to see how to create a splash screen.

1 Place a ProgressBar component (from the Win32 tab) onto your splash form.

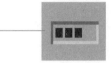

In the example, the progress bar rises in values of 25. This could be increased, say to increments of 10 showing a more gradual rise effect when the application is run.

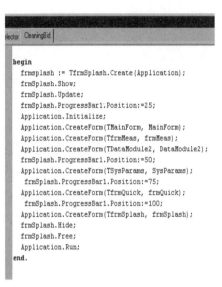

```
begin
  frmsplash := TfrmSplash.Create(Application);
  frmSplash.Show;
  frmSplash.Update;
  frmSplash.ProgressBar1.Position:=25;
  Application.Initialize;
  Application.CreateForm(TMainForm, MainForm);
  Application.CreateForm(TfrmMeas, frmMeas);
  Application.CreateForm(TDataModule2, DataModule2);
  frmSplash.ProgressBar1.Position:=50;
  Application.CreateForm(TSysParams, SysParams);
  frmSplash.ProgressBar1.Position:=75;
  Application.CreateForm(TfrmQuick, frmQuick);
  frmSplash.ProgressBar1.Position:=100;
  Application.CreateForm(TfrmSplash, frmSplash);
  frmSplash.Hide;
  frmSplash.Free;
  Application.Run;
end.
```

2 View your application's unit files and open the main project file (the one with the same name as your application).

3 As your application creates each of its forms, place lines of code in an equidistant position between form creation, changing the splash form's progress bar's Position property to values between zero and 100. This will have the effect of displaying a rising scale when your application is launched.

How the progress bar looks when the application is loading.

WindowState and focus

When designing applications using Delphi, it is essential to remember that the users may not always use your application in the exact way that you intended it. To help ensure some sort of standardisation, you can set all forms in your application to appear maximised – filling the whole screen.

You can also set the WindowState property at run-time. This can be done by including the code:

formname.Window State:=wsMaximized

(no spaces) behind the OnShow event of the form.

Change the form's WindowState property to wsMaximized. The WindowState property determines how the form will look at run-time.

Form focus

A form has focus when the user clicks on the form at run-time. In the Windows environment, providing you have not changed the screen settings, the active window shows up with the title bar appearing in blue. Only one form at any one time can have focus.

Component focus

On each form, only one component can have focus at any one time. The component with focus is easy to spot – the cursor will be flashing inside it or there will be some obvious highlighted border or dotted line around the component.

Setting component focus

To set focus to a particular component when a form is opened, the following code can be used (behind the form's OnShow event).

When the form is opened focus is passed to the edit component named edit2.

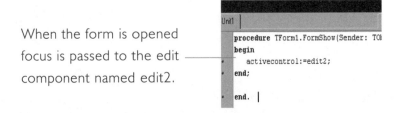

Adding a menu to a form

A menu is a great way to include many options in a neat and tidy fashion.

Menus can be used to offer users a different method of running your application or, as a way to provide further options for use.

Creating an Accounts menu

In this example you will create a typical menu for an accounts package.

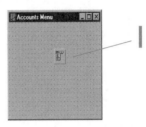

1 From the Standard tab, place a MainMenu component onto your form. Double-click on this component.

2 Enter a menu caption for the first menu option. Press enter.

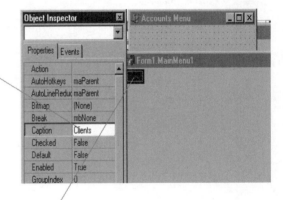

3 Click on the adjacent blue rectangle and repeat the process for more menu headings.

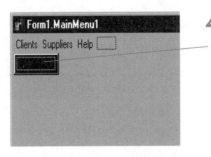

4 Add more menu items under each menu heading by clicking on the blue rectangle and amending the associated Caption property from the Object Inspector.

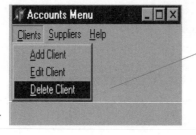

The form with menu items added.

You can preview your menu by simply pointing and clicking to the items on the form.

Adding sub-menus

A sub-menu is used where a menu item has more than one option.

Right-clicking on a menu item allows you to add further menu items as well as delete existing menu items.

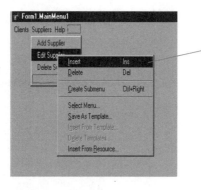

| From within the Menu Designer, select the menu item to have a sub-menu then right-click and choose Create Sub-menu.

Adding separators

A separator bar allows you to include graphical splits in your menu.

| Right-click on the menu item below where the line is to be created. Choose Insert.

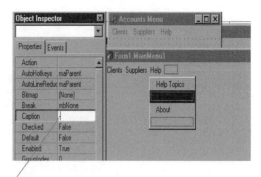

2 Place a dash in the caption property of the new item. A blank line is now included in the menu.

Adding menu events

Once you have completed the design of your menus and sub-menus the next logical activity to complete is to add some events to each menu item.

Opening a form from a menu item

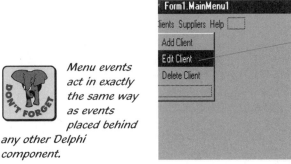

Menu events act in exactly the same way as events placed behind any other Delphi component.

1 From the Menu Designer, select a menu item where you wish to add an event.

2 Launch the Object Inspector for the menu item. Click on the Events tab.

```
procedure TForm1.EditClient1Click(Sender: T
begin
    frmedclient.showmodal;
end;

end.
```

3 Place any relevant code behind the OnClick event of the menu item.

4 Now compile and run your application. When you choose the menu item from the menu on your form, the OnClick event will run and, in this example, the form named 'frmedclient' will be opened.

Other menu features

The following features will enhance your form menus.

Adding a menu default

Each menu can have a default item. This allows you to automatically launch the OnClick event for the default item when the parent item in the menu is double-clicked.

Set the Default property to true for the menu item required to be set as the default.

2 When you run the application, double-clicking on the Clients menu will run the OnClick event behind the Edit Client menu item.

Add an image to a menu item by loading a bitmap file into the menu item's Bitmap property.

Adding a keyboard shortcut

A keyboard shortcut is a combination of keyboard depressions that can speed up menu operation (especially useful if your background is in DOS or UNIX based applications).

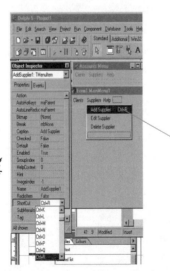

You can also add accelerator keys to menu items by adding an & in front of the character to be used in the accelerator key combination Alt+letter.

From the Object Inspector, select the Shortcut property. From the drop-down list select the appropriate keyboard shortcut for the menu item. This shortcut now appears against the item in the menu.

Adding a popup menu

A popup menu is a special type of menu that can be attached to a component behind that component's PopupMenu property. A popup menu can be used to give your users extra control over the component that currently has focus.

Using a popup menu to change a grid's font

In this example you will learn how to right-click on a grid (using a PopupMenu component) and change the Font property of that grid.

Allowing users to change the font size and style at run-time greatly enhances the flexibility of your application. This facility is particularly useful for those with sight problems who may choose to increase the font size on the screen.

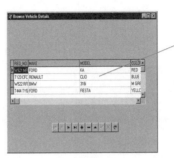

1 Add a DBGrid component to a form and link it to a dataset.

2 From the Standard component tab place a PopupMenu component onto the form.

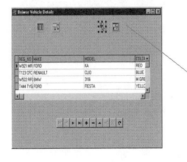

3 From the Dialogs component palette, place a FontDialog component onto the form.

The FontDialog component is used at run-time to allow users to choose a font for a particular component.

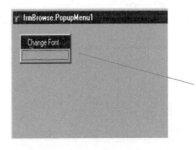

4 Double-click on the PopupMenu component and add an option through the Menu Designer.

...cont'd

The Menu Designer within the PopupMenu component works in exactly the same way as the Menu Designer in the MainMenu component.

Make the font property of the FontDialog component equal that of the DBGrid.

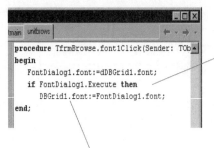

```
procedure TfrmBrowse.font1Click(Sender: TOb
begin
    FontDialog1.font:=dDBGrid1.font;
    if FontDialog1.Execute then
        DBGrid1.font:=FontDialog1.font;
end;
```

5 Place this program code behind the OnClick event of the Change Font popup menu item. (The FontDialog component is executed and the user can change the font.)

Finally, the Font property of the DBGrid is changed to reflect the new user choice.

6 Run your application and right-click on the grid. Click on the Change Font menu item.

7 A new font is chosen or the current font properties are changed.

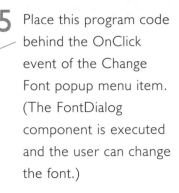

8 The grid font is changed.

Message dialogue box

So far, you've used the ShowMessage function to display information messages to your users. The MessageDlg function provides a more flexible messaging routine that allows users to make a response. An example of the function could be:

MessageDlg('Close Application. Are you sure?', mtConfirmation, [mbYes, mbNo], 0) ;

The MessageDlg function always displays the message box in the centre of your screen.

In the above function, the message displayed is followed by a value that describes the type of message being displayed (in this case a box with a blue question mark). The values in square brackets refer to the buttons that will be displayed in the box, each separated by a comma (in this case a Yes and No button). For simplicity, there will always be a zero before the last bracket. The box looks like this:

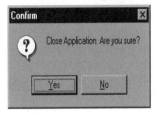

Press F1 when the cursor is on the MessageDlg word to see a complete explanation of the possible box types and button values available.

Using the MessageDlg function to process a user response

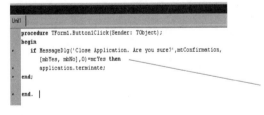

```
procedure TForm1.Button1Click(Sender: TObject);
begin
  if MessageDlg('Close Application. Are you sure?',mtConfirmation,
     [mbYes, mbNo],0)=mrYes then
       application.terminate;
end;

end.
```

If the user clicks the Yes button, mrYes is returned and the program code is carried out (application.terminate).

The MessageDlg function returns the value of the button that the user selects. There are a number of possible buttons that can be displayed.

Using an input box

An input box allows the user to enter values into a 'super' edit component on the screen. This can prove useful when you require the user to make some input. An example of the function is as follows:

InputBox('Input Response', 'Enter your name', 'Type here');

The 'Input Response' string is displayed in the title bar of the input box, the next string is displayed as the actual request within the box. The final string ('Type here') is the default text that will be displayed in the Edit component before the user makes their entry. The input box looks like this:

Using the InputBox function to capture a user's name

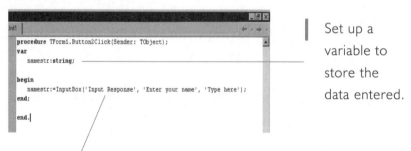

I   Set up a variable to store the data entered.

2   Display the input box with the default text in the Edit component 'Type here'. When the user enters a response, store it in the variable.

The InputBox is displayed with an OK and a Cancel button included by default.

OLE

OLE or Object Linking and Embedding is the Windows standard for allowing you to embed or link data (objects) from one application into another. Delphi's OLE container component is useful to allow you to link Microsoft Word, Excel and PowerPoint, as well as other application data, into your forms.

You could think of the OLE container as a little box that holds a different application and that, when double-clicked, allows this application to open for use.

Adding a Word document

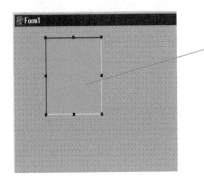

1 From the System component tab, place an OLE container component onto your form.

2 Double-click the component, or right-click and open the Insert Object dialogue box.

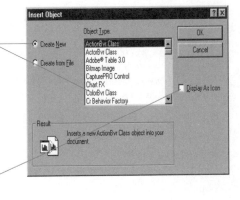

3 Choose Create New and pick a file type to include in your application.

4 If you would like the linked file's application icon to be displayed on your form, click Display As Icon.

5 Align your OLE container component with the form (client) to allow your file to be displayed in a larger area.

Rather than create a document from scratch, you can choose an existing filename.

An OLE container component could be used in a stock system to provide product specification information.

Any changes made to the embedded file from its own application are reflected when you access it through your application.

The OLE standard is supported by all the major PC application software providers.

1 Click on the Create from File option and browse and select an existing file.

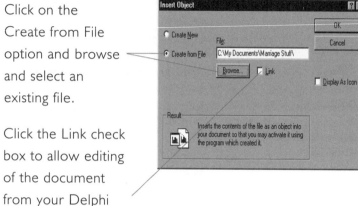

2 Click the Link check box to allow editing of the document from your Delphi application. Click OK.

3 Run your application. Double-click on the OLE container component to launch the associated file's application.

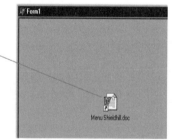

4 In this case, Microsoft Word loads and you can edit and save the file chosen in the OLE container component.

Windows standard dialogs

The Dialogs component page provides standard components available in all Windows applications. These common dialog components ensure that you provide a standard interface which your users will recognise.

When carrying out basic Windows operations – Open, Save, Print etc. – you should always use the components available in the Dialogs component page. This ensures that your application follows the Windows standard.

Creating a basic word processor application

In this example, you will use the OpenDialog and SaveDialog component to create a word processor that allows the viewing and editing of simple text documents.

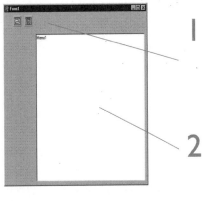

1 From the Dialogs component page, place an OpenDialog and SaveDialog component onto your form.

2 Place a Memo component onto the form. This will be used to display loaded files.

Change the ScrollBars property of the memo component to show vertical scrollbars. This will make it easier to view large files.

3 Change the OpenDialog's DefaultExt property to txt. This will cause the application to append the txt extension to files that don't have it already. Change the InitialDir property to start the load process from the C drive's root directory.

4 Repeat step three for the process for the SaveDialog component.

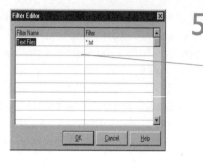

5 For the OpenDialog and SaveDialog component, choose the Filter property and name and list the files to be included when the dialogs are run.

Loading a large file may cause an error to appear as the Memo component Lines property is limited in size.

6 Add two buttons to your form. Change the Caption properties to reflect Load and Save buttons.

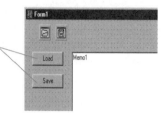

7 Add the following code behind the OnClick event of the buttons.

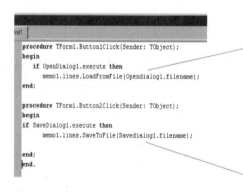

```
procedure TForm1.Button1Click(Sender: TObject);
begin
    if OpenDialog1.execute then
        memo1.lines.LoadFromFile(Opendialog1.filename);
end;

procedure TForm1.Button2Click(Sender: TObject);
begin
if SaveDialog1.execute then
    memo1.lines.SaveToFile(Savedialog1.filename);

end;
end.
```

The Load button. Carries out a file open and populates the memo component with the file loaded.

The Save button. Carries out a file save and writes contents of the memo component to the file.

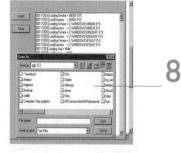

8 Run your application. The Save option is shown here.

Data-Aware Components

In this chapter you will find out a bit more about data-aware components and how these can be linked to a dataset to make database programming purposeful and straightforward. Data-aware components can be found in the Data Controls page.

Covers

Chapter Ten

The DßText component

The DBText component is the data-aware version of the common Label component. It simply allows you to attach data to a label for display purposes.

Set the AutoSize property of the DBText component to True to ensure that all your data will be printed.

Displaying a customer balance

In this example, the DBDEMOS customer table has its Company and Contact fields displayed using DBText components.

To view all organisation and contact details, add a DBNavigator component and hook it up to your data source.

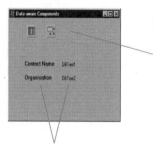

1 Add a Table and DataSource component and hook them up to the customer table in the DBDEMOS database.

2 Place and name two label components and place two DBText components.

You can only link each DBText component with one data field at any one time.

3 Attach each DBText component to the data source on the form.

4 Attach a field from the table field list provided. This is the field data that will be displayed in the DBText component when the application is run.

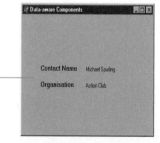

5 Run your application. The first record in the customer table will be displayed.

The DBEdit component

Whilst the DBText component allows you to display field data, the DBEdit component goes a stage further and allows you to edit that data.

Editing a customer contact name
In this example, the DBDEMOS customer table is set to allow editing of the customer contact detail.

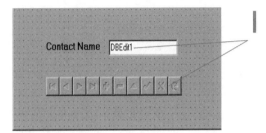

1 Add a Table and a DBEdit component to your form. Add a DBNavigator component.

2 Hook the DataSource and DataField properties to the form's DataSource and Contact field.

3 Hook the DBNavigator's data source up to the main form's data source.

Change the DBEdit component's ReadOnly property to True to stop users amending table data.

4 Traverse through the contact details making any amendments to the names displayed.

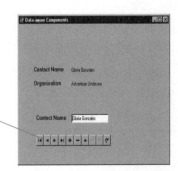

You must move to the next record to save any changes made.

The DBMemo component

The DBMemo component is used to edit or display a string data field that contains a large amount of data. This field allows you to display field data on multiple lines.

Displaying venue details
In this example, a DBMemo component is used to display remarks about venue locations for events. The table used is Venues and it can be found in the DBDEMOS database.

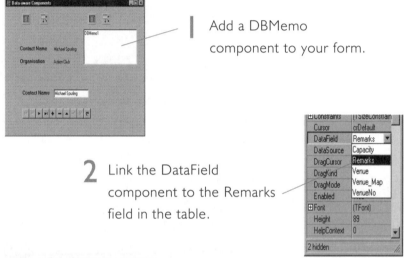

Add a DBMemo component to your form.

2 Link the DataField component to the Remarks field in the table.

3 When your application is run, the details of the Remarks field are displayed over a number of lines.

4 Change the ScrollBars property of the DBMemo component to allow very large field data to be displayed easily.

The DBListBox component

The DBListBox component allows the user to change the contents of a field by choosing a new value from a list of choices provided.

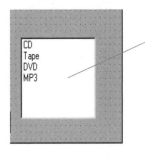

1 Add a DBListBox component to your form.

2 Link the DataField component to a suitable field (in this case Media_Type).

3 In the Items property of the DBListBox component, list the items from which the user can choose.

The DBComboBox operates in a similar fashion to the DBListBox.

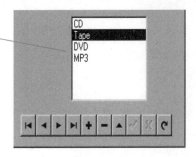

4 Add and hook up to a DataSource and DBNavigator component.

5 When you run your application, the value stored in the Media_Type field for each record in the table is highlighted in blue. Use your mouse to click and replace this field with a different list entry.

The DBCheckBox component

The DBCheckBox component is used when you want to control a table field containing a Boolean value. The DBCheckBox component is ideally suited to the job, as it has only two states, True or False (on/off , stop/go etc.).

Sending a venue brochure
In this example, if the DBCheckBox is checked (ticked), then a brochure will be sent to the customer.

If the field type of the field used in the DBCheckBox component is logical then the ValueChecked and ValueUnChecked properties have no effect on the underlying data – ValueChecked will always contain 'True' and ValueUnChecked will always contain 'False'.

| Add a DBCheckBox component to your form.

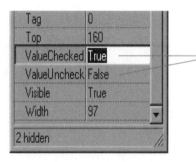

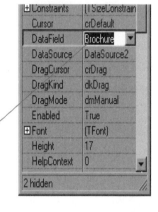

2 Hook this component up to a suitable DataSource and DataField.

Set the AllowGrayed property option to True if you wish the DBCheckBox to have a greyed state.

3 The values entered here will determine what is then stored in the actual table field when the user either checks or unchecks the DBCheckBox component.

4 Change the Caption property to a suitable description and run your application. Successive mouse clicks change the state of the DBCheckBox component.

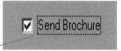

The DBRadioGroup component

The DBRadioGroup component is used when you want to allow the user to choose only one option from a list.

Determining the maximum cost

In this example, the DBRadioGroup component is used to display maximum costs.

The contents of the Items property and the Values property in the DBGroupBox are related by their physical position in each list. You must ensure that the values listed are the ones that you want written back to your table.

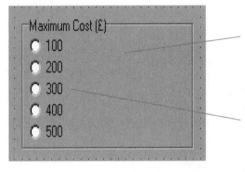

1 Place a DBRadioGroup component onto your form.

2 Amend the Caption property and list the choices for the group in the Items property.

3 In the Values property, list the corresponding values that will be written back to your table.

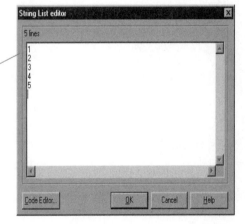

4 Run your application. The selected value can be changed by clicking with your mouse.

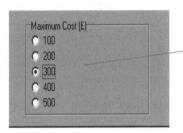

The DBImage component

BLOB stands for Binary Large OBject.

The DBImage component is used where your database tables contain BLOB data. In normal use this component is used to display images from database records.

Displaying animal images

In this example, a table of animal information includes an image in each record. The DBImage component is used to display each image. This example uses the Animal table in the DBDEMOS database.

When designing applications, BLOB data gives you a fantastic opportunity to include visual images. This works very well when you are writing applications that rely on images such as a fashion catalogue application.

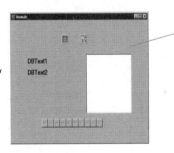

1 Place two DBText components, a DBNavigator component and a DBImage component on a form.

2 Hook up all the data-aware components to a data source linked to the Animal table.

3 Link the DBImage DataField component to the BMP field, and the two DBText components to the NAME and AREA fields.

4 When you run your application, the image is displayed in the DBImage component from the underlying data file. Use the Next button on the DBNavigator bar to move through the records and view the other animal images.

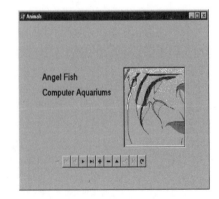

The DBLookupComboBox component

The DBLookupComboBox component is similar to a standard DBComboBox component. However, with a DBLookupComboBox component, you can display field values in the combo box that come from another dataset. This allows you to maintain separate lookup tables containing values that can be used within your application.

This example shows the amendment of one record. In a live application, to save the data you would require to move to the next record in the table or issue a command to post the changes back to the database.

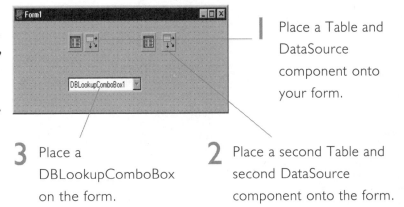

I Place a Table and DataSource component onto your form.

3 Place a DBLookupComboBox on the form.

2 Place a second Table and second DataSource component onto the form.

4 Link both tables with a corresponding data source.

5 Click on the DBLookupComboBox component and open its Object Inspector. Link the DataSource and DataField properties to the first data source that you placed. The DataField is the field that will receive the choice the user picks from the DBLookupComboBox at run-time.

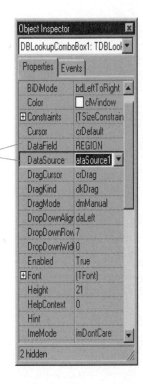

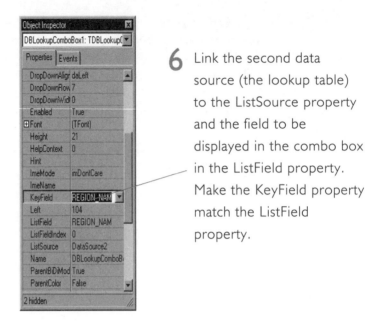

6 Link the second data source (the lookup table) to the ListSource property and the field to be displayed in the combo box in the ListField property. Make the KeyField property match the ListField property.

Now, when you run your application and click on the combo box, you are presented with a list of values from an independent data table from which you make a choice. This value chosen is saved back to the record in the main dataset.

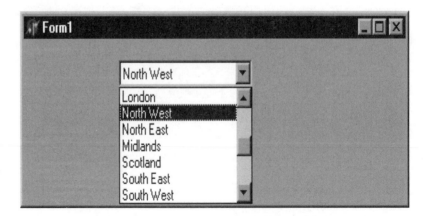

You can use the DBLookupListBox component in a similar way to the DBLookupComboBox component. The only difference is that a list is provided rather than a clickable combo box for the user to make a choice from.

Common Errors

In this chapter you will look at the errors that can commonly occur when developing Delphi applications. You'll learn a bit more about variable types and learn how to use the debugger effectively.

Covers

Chapter Eleven

Compilation error messages

All programmers make mistakes. When you are writing lines and lines of program code in various units and procedures and using numerous commands, functions and variables, things are sure to go wrong. The Delphi compiler checks your programs each time you compile them and reports any errors to you.

When debugging your program it is often advisable to turn Optimization off. This will ensure that every line of code is available for you when you carry out line by line program code checks.

Setting compiler options

From the Project, Options menu, you can see the Compiler tab to view the settings used when compiling projects.

Selecting Optimization ensures that the code generated after compilation will run as fast as possible.

If you are not an expert, it's best to leave the Compiler options set to their default values.

Messages offer you hints and warnings which can prove useful when designing applications.

Common errors

The following errors are those that you will often come across when compiling your Delphi project.

To compile your project, choose Compile from the Project menu. To run your project choose Run from the Run menu.

Incorrect syntax

The compiler stops compilation and highlights the line where the error occurs.

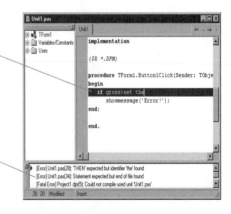

Tips are given as to the likely cause of the error (in this case the 'then' is misspelt).

Missing variables

This error often occurs when you are working with a number of variables – it is very easy to omit one from the variable declaration.

When an error appears, highlight its detail and press F1. Help for the error will be displayed.

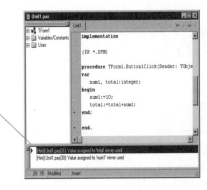

Here, the variable total is missing from the variable declaration.

The complier advises you that there is an undeclared identifier giving you a hint which can help rectify the problem.

Hints

Hints also give you information that should prove useful in the drive towards designing your program well.

Here, a hint is provided to let you know the variable is never used in the program therefore this might alert you to question why it is included in the program code.

Understanding variable types

It is important when designing applications that you choose variable types that match the use that you will be making of the variable. For example choosing an integer variable to store a person's surname would cause problems and would result in an error.

It is also common to make mistakes when assigning variables that are to be used in some arithmetic calculations.

Check your program code by hand before compiling it – look specifically for type mismatches.

Dividing integers

In this example one integer variable is divided by another. Look at the compiler error.

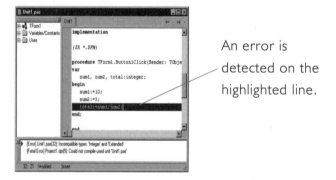

An error is detected on the highlighted line.

The program code is attempting to divide two integer numbers that do not result in a whole number answer (10 divided by 3 gives an answer of 3.33). Of course, the variable total should have been declared as a real (or some other float) type.

In this example an integer is incorrectly assigned to a string variable.

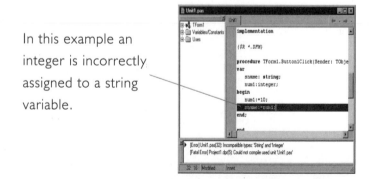

Using the debugger

The debugger is a powerful feature in the Delphi IDE that allows you to find and fix any bugs that might exist in your program code. The debugger tools make finding difficult logic errors easy to solve by opening a 'window' into the actual line by line operation of your program code. Debugger options are found in the Run menu.

The Step Over menu item allows you to see your program code being executed one line at a time.

Your program can include as many breakpoints as required. To run to the next breakpoint, press the Run button on the toolbar when the program stops at each breakpoint.

Adding a watch allows you to follow the values that are stored in variables at run-time.

Adding a breakpoint

A breakpoint is a big stop sign that instructs the program to stop at the highlighted point in the program code.

To delete a breakpoint, click on that breakpoint in the margin and the red highlighted line will disappear.

To add a breakpoint, click in the left margin next to the line of code you wish to stop at – the line is highlighted in red.

Stepping over your code

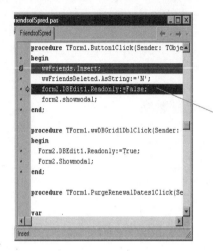

1 From the Run menu, run your project.

2 Your program will run as normal until it reaches the first breakpoint.

Stepping through your program code is an excellent way to learn exactly how each line of program code is evaluated.

3 You can run the project by pressing F9. Or press F8 to step through each line of code (watching the logic).

Adding a watch

You can view the value of a variable at run-time by placing your mouse over the variable at a breakpoint or during Step Over.

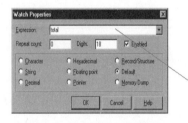

1 From the Run menu choose Add Watch.

2 Type in the variable or expression to be watched.

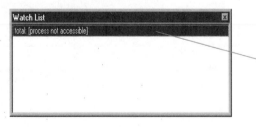

3 Run your program. View the watch at any breakpoint or during Step Over.

Tips For Experts

This chapter will introduce you to a number of useful features that will enhance your applications. As well as this, you will also learn some of the secrets of professional programming.

Covers

Chapter Twelve

Creating a data module

A data module is a repository where you can store, in one area, all the tables that your application uses. Data modules take the hassle out of working with data and take away the need to use Table components and DataSource components on every form requiring data manipulation on it.

Creating a data module

From the File, New menu, choose the data module object and double-click.

As you name your data module and use a database and table, notice that the tree structure to the right of the main window changes to reflect the data chosen.

2 Rename the data module.

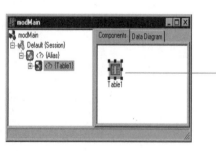

The Table component can be found on the Data Access tab.

3 Place a Table component onto the data module.

4 Launch the Object Inspector for the table, and name the table.

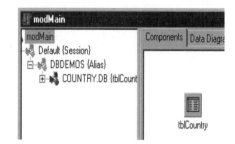

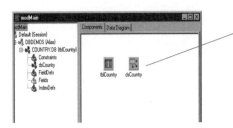

5 Add a data source to your data module and hook this up to the table (tblCountry).

When you use the data module in your form, all the Table and DataSource components instantly become available to you to use.

6 Save your Delphi project naming the data module as datam.pas (or any other suitable name).

Using the data module

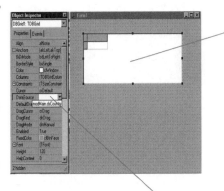

I Add a DBGrid to a form. From the File menu, choose the Use Unit menu option and select the data module you just created.

When you hook up the data source to the grid, no data appears. This is because the table component in the data module's Active property is set to False.

2 Click on the DataSource property of the DBGrid and choose the data source from your data module to hook up to the grid.

3 Open your data module and set the table's Active property to True.

4 The DBGrid component should now display your data from the data module.

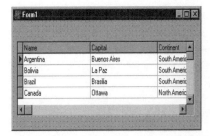

Using your data module

Once you have successfully created a data module for your application, the components in it can be used anywhere in your application. This ensures that your programs are easy to maintain as all the data for the application is neatly contained in one area.

Programmers and software developers often include complex program code in their applications. This is often unnecessary and can be replaced by straightforward logical, simple code. Always remember that you might not be the person responsible for maintaining your application – therefore clarity and ease of understanding should be paramount at the design stage.

Viewing the country table

To open the form created previously you need to add a new form to your application and place a button on it.

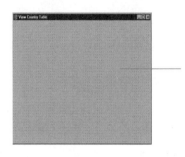

1 Add a new form and change the form Caption and Name properties.

Right-click on the Start button and choose the Find utility. Look for 'buttons' and this should help identify a folder where button images are stored and can be used.

2 From the Additional tab, place a BitBtn component on the form. Add an image to this button by loading it in the Glyph property of the button.

3 Behind the OnClick event for the BitBtn, show your form with the grid on it.

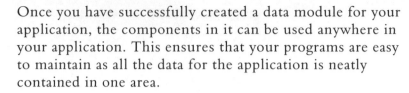

```
procedure TForm4.BitBtn1Click(Sender: TObject);
begin
  frmViewcountry.showmodal;
end;

end.
```

4 Run your application.

Creating a custom component page

Many third party software companies sell component add-ons to the component palette shipped with Delphi. These components often enhance the existing Delphi components and provide an easy means to carry out often complex tasks.

As you build applications using Delphi you will use many of the available components. You may even add component libraries to Delphi from a third party. This all adds up to an array of components held in a number of component tabs. To ease the confusion, create a custom component page and place in here all the components that you frequently use.

Adding a new component page

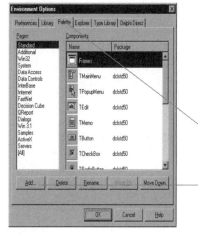

1 From the Tools menu choose the Environment Options menu item.

2 Select the Palette tab.

3 Click Add and name the new page. Click OK.

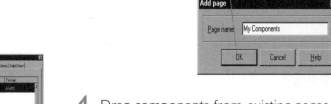

Use the MoveUp and Move Down buttons to rearrange your components on your custom page.

4 Drag components from existing pages to your new page. Click OK when you are finished.

5 View the new component page.

Indexing tables at run-time

When you distribute your Delphi applications they are out of your control. Events such as switching a PC off when your application is live, or a power failure can cause database index files to be corrupt and your application to fail. It is good practice to include a 'fix' menu item, button, or separate application which will recreate index files in the event of a problem.

Index files are set up to allow you to order your data in a specific manner. Each table can have many index files and these are created either in Database Desktop or in a commercial database application.

Recreating a table with two index files

1 Add a button to your form, or a menu item and change the caption to 'Database Fix'.

2 Behind the OnClick event add the following program code.

Before re-indexing a table you must ensure that it is not open anywhere in the application. This might mean (if you haven't used a data module) listing a number of close statements in the code.

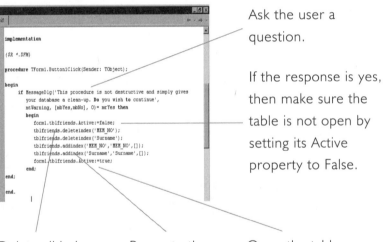

Ask the user a question.

If the response is yes, then make sure the table is not open by setting its Active property to False.

You should note that the syntax of the 'AddIndex' function is (with no line break):

tablename.addindex('Index File Name','Index Field',[]);

Delete all index files associated with the table.

Recreate the index files for the table.

Open the table ready for use.

3 Run your application and re-index your table.

Adding comments

Your finished applications will be made up of many lines of program code held in many units. Whilst you understand what each procedure in your program does, it might be harder for others to understand or even for you to understand at a later date. Comments are an excellent way to ensure your program code is readable and understandable.

You can replace the brace comments using a left parenthesis followed by an asterisk i.e. (* to start a comment, and an asterisk followed by a right parenthesis i.e. *) to end a comment.

Method 1

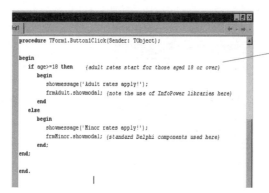

All comments shown between the left and right brace (and displayed in blue) are comments and are ignored by the compiler.

Method 2

Add comments to your program code as you build it. Programmers rarely revisit their code and place useful comments!

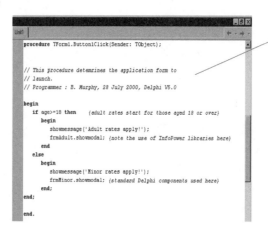

Use the double slash // to make a complete comment a line. This is handy to use at the start of procedures to describe the purpose of the code included.

Comments add absolutely no overhead to your completed application. You can be sure that your application will run without difficulty and just as fast with or without comments.

Creating an About screen

All professional Windows-based applications have an About screen included, which usually gives you some detail about the product, its version and contact numbers for further help. You can create an About screen easily using the MainMenu component and the Memo component found in the Standard component page.

Although the menu has details of help topics and shortcuts, these are not explained here.

| Add a MainMenu component to your form. Double-click it and open the Menu Designer.

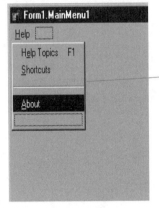

2 Add the menu items shown. Remember to include a shortcut (F1) for the Help Topics menu item and include a separator line between the Shortcuts and About menu items.

To add a new form to your application, choose the New Form menu item from the File menu.

3 Add and name a new form to your application.

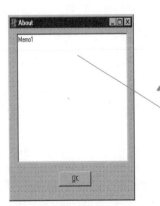

4 Add a Memo component and a Button component to the new form. Choose an appropriate caption for the form and for the button.

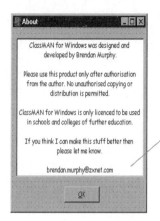

Remember to set the Memo component's ReadOnly property to True. This will stop users from changing the text included in the message.

5 Add some text to the Lines property of the Memo component. Align the text by amending the component's Alignment property. Change the font to Comic Sans MS by amending the Font property.

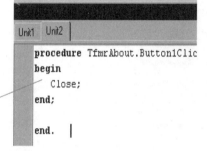

To move between forms at design-time, choose the View Form icon or press Shift+F12.

6 Add this code behind the button's OnClick event to close the form when the button is pressed.

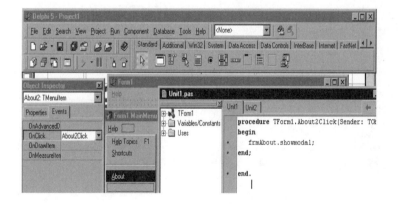

7 From the Menu Designer in the MainMenu component, show the form behind the OnClick event of the About menu item.

8 Run your application and choose the About menu item. Click OK when you've read the message.

Programmer tips

Don't be afraid to space your program out with plenty of blank lines between code blocks. This will also help increase readability.

Run a pencil line between a 'begin' and its corresponding 'end' or an IF statement or a control loop. If your pencil cuts through any code on the way, then your indentation isn't correct.

There are many differing views on programming standards. A common view is that all reserved words (those provided by the language) be typed in upper case, with user-defined variables being typed in lower case.

Great programming comes from practice and the adoption of standards that make your code professional in design. Already you've looked at comments which enhance the readability and maintenance of your code. Two further areas are worth consideration, namely meaningful variable names and proper indentation.

Meaningful variable names

Always ensure that your variable names are easily identifiable with the data that they are declared to store. For example, if you are setting up a variable that will hold a person's surname then 'sname' would be better than x or y as a suitable variable name.

Meaningful names should extend to your components and forms. Decide on a standard and stick to it.

Indentation

Indentation makes the logic of your program stand out and increases readability. A good rule of thumb is to indent three spaces where appropriate.

An example program

The following program code illustrates the above points:

In this program a table is read from the first record to the last record and a total is calculated.

Distributing Your Application

In this chapter, you'll learn how to package your application up into a neat bundle for easy distribution.

Covers

Chapter Thirteen

InstallShield Express

InstallShield Express is widely used and can be found with most Windows-based applications.

InstallShield Express is a powerful package that allows you to distribute your completed Delphi applications easily. InstallShield Express packages all the files your application needs into one neat bundle which can then be distributed on floppy disk.

Installing the program

InstallShield Express comes with Delphi and can be installed by inserting the Delphi CD into your PC.

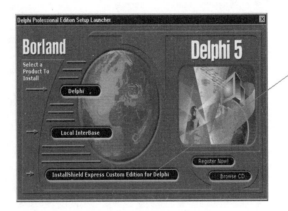

Click on the installation button and follow through the guided instructions.

Opening InstallShield Express

To open the package choose it from the Program menu on the Start button.

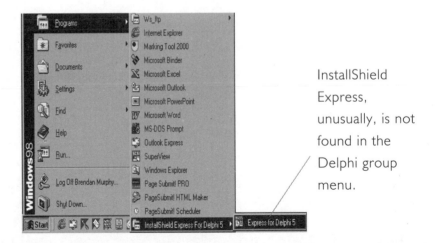

InstallShield Express, unusually, is not found in the Delphi group menu.

Creating a new setup project

Each time you want to distribute your Delphi application you must setup a new InstallShield Express project.

Always give your application a brand name. This helps give it an identity and can help when you are looking to develop the product commercially as well as helping users to associate more fully with your application.

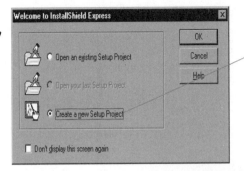

| Choose the Create a new Setup Project option.

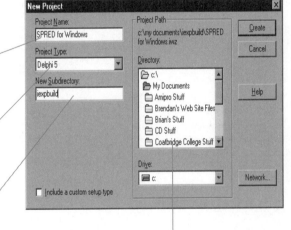

2 Enter the name of your application.

3 Enter your project type.

If you want to store your InstallShield Express file on a network click on the Network button.

4 Enter a new sub-directory to create the distributable InstallShield Express file.

5 If you don't want to create a new sub-directory to hold your InstallShield Express file then choose an appropriate folder from the ones listed.

Choosing setup options

The Setup Checklist allows you to determine how your completed InstallShield Express files will look.

Choose each subheading in a sequential order when building your InstallShield Express distribution files.

The Setup Checklist gives a visual overview of the status of your InstallShield Express setup.

You must not leave the Application Name, Version or Company fields blank otherwise your application will be unable to uninstall through the Windows Add/Remove Programs utility.

Here, identify your application's name, its executable file, the version, your company name and the directory you want the application to install to on your user's PC.

2 Choose the Main Window tab to change the display of your setup application. Choose the Features tab and ensure that your application is setup to be uninstalled on your user's PC should they decide to do this.

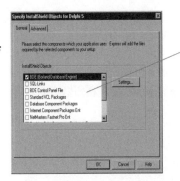

If your application uses aliases then these must be created when you check the BDE (Borland Database Engine) check box otherwise your application won't run on its destination machine.

3 Add any objects that your application uses. In particular you are likely to use the Borland BDE and QuickReport Component Packages.

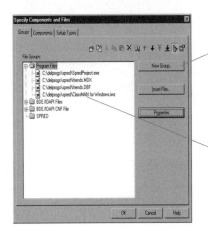

4 Create a group for your application to be installed in.

5 Choose all the files required to be distributed with your application. This will include database tables and indexes.

6 The Select User Interface components and Make Registry Changes checklist entries can be left at their default values.

7 Enter the .EXE file to be run to launch your application. Leave the Run Command Parameters blank and enter a description to be displayed underneath your application icon.

Running the Disk Builder

Once you have completed the setup process using InstallShield Wizard you can run the Disk Builder to create the disks required to distribute your application.

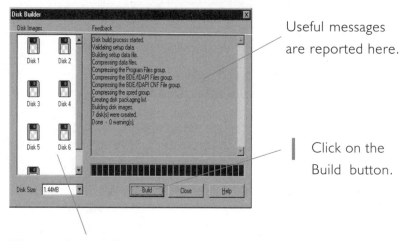

Useful messages are reported here.

Click on the Build button.

The number of disks required to distribute your application is shown.

Testing the installation

Once you have successfully built your distribution disks you can test the installation application to ensure that it works.

Click on the Test Run option.

2 You will be guided through the familiar Windows application setup process.

Creating distribution media

Once your installation application is complete and has been tested, you are ready to copy the setup files to disk.

Ensure that your donor PC is virus free ensuring that you do not infect other machines when you distribute your application.

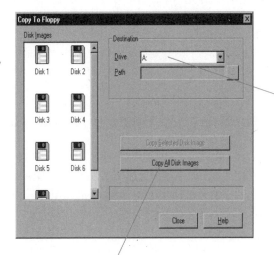

| Choose the floppy drive (A) or another sub-directory in which to store your completed installation application.

2 Click on the Copy All Disk Images button.

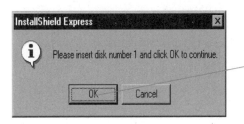

3 Insert blank formatted floppy disks and copy your installation application to disk ready for distribution.

4 A message is displayed to alert you when the copying process is complete.

Windows guidelines

For further information on the Windows logo requirements visit:

http://www.msdn.microsoft. com/winlogo/.

When you build your applications for distribution, you can be guaranteed that InstallShield Wizard conforms to the requirements of Microsoft Windows logo requirements. Windows logo requirements allow you to use the Windows logo on your applications provided you conform to a set of standards. Use of the logo will also give your users confidence that your product has been tested to ensure compatibility with Windows.

Summary guidelines for Window logo compatibility

*   Keep a check on the number of icons that you have in your application group. It's best to keep the number of icons for your applications, help files and associated utilities down to a minimum. This will reduce the confusion often associated with having to make a choice from a number of options.

*   Your application should have the ability to easily uninstall. If you install your application using InstallShield Wizard then you completely conform to the Windows logo requirement to have comprehensive uninstallation capabilities.

*   Avoid changing setup files. The amendment of win.ini, config.sys and autoexec.bat files should not be done by your application.

The above summary gives you a taster of the requirements for becoming authorised to use the Windows logo. If you are looking to sell you application commercially then it is recommended that you spend some time familiarising yourself with the detailed requirements of this registration. Professional developers can gain a great marketing tool by employing this standard and, with the continued domination of Microsoft, it could become more and more popular in the near future.

Building a Database Application

In this chapter you'll look at building a complete database application from start to finish. You will use many of the components learned in Chapter Thirteen as well as learning the common structure of database applications.

Covers

Chapter Fourteen

Creating a new application

When you start Delphi, the first thing you want to do is create a new application.

Create a separate folder for each new application that you build. This will make it easier to maintain each application in the future as well as avoid problems associated with overwriting files by mistake.

Choose New Application from the File menu.

When you create a new Delphi project, you are presented with the default form, or main form, for the application. This will be the first form that your users will see when they run the application.

The main form for your application should clearly provide the users with a route to access all functional areas of the application.

The main form

It is a good idea to maximise the main form in your application. This will ensure that your application fills the user's screen when run.

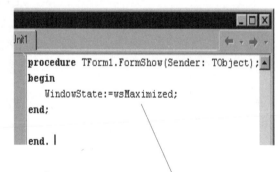

Always use meaningful names when naming files.

Place this code behind the OnShow or OnActivate event of the main form.

2 From the File menu, choose the Save Project As option and save your project to a newly created folder.

Adding components

Now, you will add some buttons to the main form to control access to your application. You will also add a panel to make the main form look more attractive.

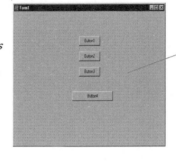

You can add accelerator keys to each button by including an & before the letter to act as the accelerator key.

Add four buttons to the main form (from the Standard tab).

Multi-select a group of components, right-click and align them easily.

2 Amend the size of each button and add meaningful caption text. Change the Name property of each button to reflect a suitable name.

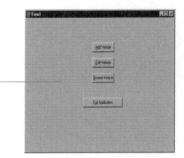

3 Behind the OnClick event for the Exit Application button place the following program code.

The MessageDlg function displays a message dialogue box on the screen with two buttons.

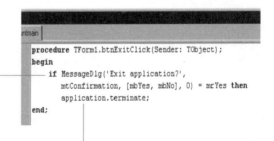

```
procedure TForm1.btnExitClick(Sender: TObject);
begin
  if MessageDlg('Exit application?',
     mtConfirmation, [mbYes, mbNo], 0) = mrYes then
     application.terminate;
end;
```

If the user chooses the Yes button then mrYes is returned from the function, and the application is terminated using application.terminate.

Browsing vehicle details

Now that the main form has been created you will create the next simplest form. This form will be used to browse vehicle details in a grid.

 The 'vehicle.dbf' file doesn't exist. Create it using Database Desktop and store it in the DBDEMOS database. Add your own vehicle data.

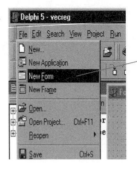

I From the File menu, choose the New Form menu option.

2 Change the Caption and Name property of the new form to reflect its purpose.

3 From the Data Access component tab, add a Table and a DataSource component.

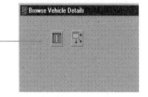

4 Hook the table component up to the file vehicle.dbf in its TableName property.

5 Link the DataSource component to the dataset by assigning the DataSet property in the DataSource component.

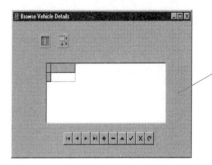

6 From the Data Controls component tab, place a DBGrid and DBNavigator component onto your form.

7 Hook the DBGrid and DBNavigator component up to the DataSource component on the form. Do this by assigning the DataSource property of each of the components.

8 Set the Table component's Active property to True and the grid should populate with table data. Resize the grid's overall size and column width to create an acceptable view of the data.

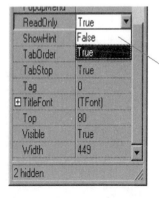

9 Change the ReadOnly property of the DBGrid component to True to stop users amending data in this view.

Amending vehicle details

Now that you can easily browse through vehicle details, the next logical step is to be able to edit these details.

1 Add a new form and amend the Caption and Name property to suit.

In a data edit/ entry form there will be a number of Label and Edit components. Spend some time aligning these components when you create the form as this helps make the form look professional to users.

2 Add a Table and DataSource component and hook these up to your data table (vehicle.dbf).

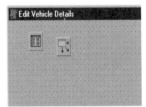

3 Add some Label components to this form as well as some DBEdit components from the Data Controls tab. Align Label components with their corresponding DBEdit components.

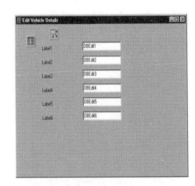

4 Change the font size of the Label components, change their Caption property and rename the DBEdit components.

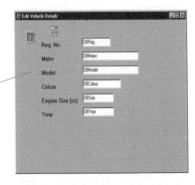

5 Attach each DBEdit component to the relevant field in the form's data source.

6 Set the Table component's Active property to True and view a complete record on the screen. Amend the width of the DBEdit components to suit the individual field data.

7 Add two standard buttons to your form. Change the Caption property of the first button to read Save and the Caption property of the second button to read Cancel.

8 For each button, set the ShowHint property to True and place a suitable hint in the Hint property of each button.

Saving and cancelling changes

The Save and Cancel buttons will be used to allow the user to make a decision whether to save any changes made to the current record or discard those changes.

When using a DBGrid component to edit data, changes are posted when the user moves to another row in the grid.

The Save button (OnClick event)

In each of the events, 'Close' follows the Post and Cancel methods. This simply closes the current form and returns you to the main menu.

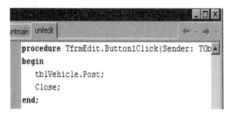

The Post method writes any changes made to the current record back to the database.

The Cancel button (OnClick event)

The Cancel method stops the changes made to the current record from being made permanent.

Moving records

You can move through records in a table by calling the First, Next, Last and Prior procedures in the OnClick event of a button (one per button).

Examples

tblVehicle.Next   —   moves forward one record
tblVehicle.Prior   —   moves back one record
tblVehicle.First   —   moves to the start of the table
tblVehicle.Last   —   moves to the end of the table

Confirming a cancel request

The Save and Cancel buttons are of a similar size and colour and they are placed right next to each other on the form. This could lead to users making a mistake and cancelling any changes that they really meant to save. You can add some program code that will give them a second chance to cancel.

The OnClick event of the Cancel button

Move the program code on this page behind the form's OnCloseQuery event and simply issue a Close behind the Cancel button. This will mean that the user will be questioned whether he presses the Cancel button or closes the form from the system menu.

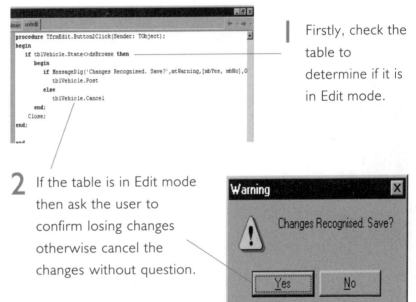

Firstly, check the table to determine if it is in Edit mode.

2 If the table is in Edit mode then ask the user to confirm losing changes otherwise cancel the changes without question.

The State property

The State property allows you to determine the current operating status of a table (dataset). As you work through your application, a table's State will change depending on what operation you are carrying out. When you open a table, State changes from 'dsInactive' to become 'dsBrowse'. When you edit data, the State changes to 'dsEdit' therefore this is a great way of checking whether the user has made changes to the data. When you post changes to a dataset or insert a record, State changes from its current status back to 'dsBrowse'. Closing a table returns State to 'dsInactive'.

Adding a new record

As well as editing existing records in a database, you are likely to want to add new ones. In the vehicle example, you are likely to want to add new vehicles to your table.

Unlike the previous two menu options, adding a new record doesn't require you to create a new form. This time you simply place an extra line of program code behind the Add Vehicle button in the main menu.

It is not necessary to issue an Insert before opening the form. You could have placed this code behind the OnShow or OnActivate event of the form, frmVehicle.

```
procedure TfrmMainMenu.btnAddVehicleClick(S
begin
    frmEdit.tblVehicle.Insert;
    frmEdit.ShowModal;
end;

end.
```

| You insert a blank record into a table by issuing Insert.

2 As the dataset is on the frmVehicle form, you are required to place this form name before the tblVehicle.Insert otherwise the table would not be found.

As the Add and Edit Vehicle options use the same form, the caption for the form should reflect the operation that is currently being carried out. At design-time leave the form's Caption property blank and then amend the main menu buttons as follows.

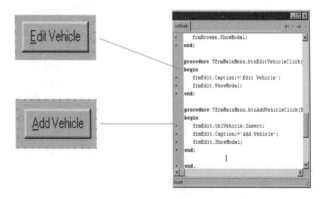

Adding finishing touches

Now that the basic functionality of your application is complete, you can add some professional touches that will make your application look more professional to your users.

Adding a Panel to the main menu

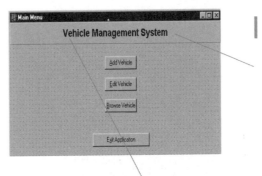

1 Add a Panel component to your main form. Align this panel to the top of your form.

Visual, or cosmetic, enhancements to a system, are best left until the main functionality of the system is operational. Essentially these extras only affect the overall look of the application.

2 Add an appropriate caption to the panel and amend the font type and size.

Adding a company logo

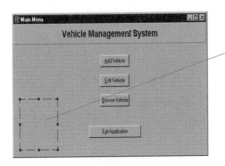

1 Add an Image component to your main form and place it towards the bottom left corner of the form.

2 Load an appropriate image into the Picture property of the Image component. Run your application.

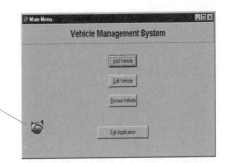

Adding a menu

A MainMenu component can be added to the main form of the application to allow a different method of accessing the application as well as to include options not available anywhere else in the application such as information about the developer or help screens.

Although the panel is aligned to the top of the form, the MainMenu component overrules this and sandwiches itself between the top of the form and the panel.Text.

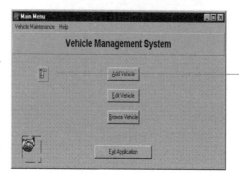

Add a MainMenu component to your main form.

These menu items duplicate the operation of the main menu buttons.

2 Include the following menu items.

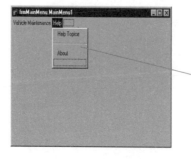

These menu items introduce options not found anywhere else in the application.

You should spend some time determining a style that suits your operation. If you make this style a standard then it will make future application development somewhat more straightforward.

Index